INCREDIBLE
CONSTRUCTIONS

INCREDIBLE CONSTRUCTIONS

and the people who built them

Mel Boring

Drawings by Sharon Farricker

Walker and Company
NEW YORK

To my brother, Doug, with love.
He taught me how to build things.

Walker's American History Series for Young People
Frances Nankin, Series Editor

ACKNOWLEDGMENTS

A book is never one person's construction; many people helped with this one.
Special thanks go to the reference library staff of the Santa Barbara, California,
Central Library, including William Richardson, Head Reference Librarian,
and Ken Warfield, Judy Pritikin, Myra Nicholas and Lee Davis, who verified
dozens of facts for this book.

Book design by Angela Foote

First published in the United States of America
by the Walker Publishing Company, Inc.
Published simultaneously in Canada by John Wiley & Sons
Canada, Limited, Rexdale, Ontario.

Library of Congress Cataloging in Publication Data
Boring, Mel, 1939–
Incredible constructions.
(Walker's American history series for young people)
Bibliography: p.
Includes index.
Summary Describes the building of ten constructions spanning 500 years of American
history. Includes the Mesa Verde cliff dwellings, the Washington Monument,
the Holland Tunnel, the Mount Rushmore carvings, and the Mackinac Bridge.
1. Building—History—Juvenile literature.   2. Civil engineering—History—
Juvenile literature.   [1. Building —History.   2. Civil engineering—History]   I. Title.
TH149.B67   1984   620   84-19552
ISBN 0-8027-6560-2 (lib. bdg.)

Printed in the United States of America
10 9 8 7 6 5 4 3 2 1

Contents

Introduction   *Awesome Achievements*   1

1. Prehistoric High-Rise Apartments   *The Cliff Dwellings*   3

2. Uncle Sam's Highway   *The National Road*   11

3. A Fight to the Finish   *The Washington Monument*   21

4. Miss Liberty   *The Statue of Liberty*   29

5. The Big Ditch   *The Panama Canal*   37

6. Underwater Wonder   *The Holland Tunnel*   46

7. Taming the Raging Red   *The Hoover Dam*   53

8. Mountain Carving   *Mount Rushmore and the Crazy Horse Monument*   61

9. Big Mac   *The Mackinac Bridge*   68

10. Treasure from Throwaways   *The Watts Towers*   79

INDEX   89

Introduction:
Awesome Achievements

*H*ow would you choose the ten most incredible constructions out of the hundreds of thousands of buildings, bridges, tunnels, canals, dams and monuments in the United States? The constructions in this book were chosen because they seemed the most impossible to build and because the people who built them were most remarkable persons. Each of these constructions makes you feel a little like an ant next to an anthill — you wonder how it could have been done, just as you wonder how tiny ants can build a mound that is hundreds of times as tall as they are.

If you have ever wondered how something was built, you are going to enjoy this book. You may want to thumb through it and look at the pictures. Some pictures show how the constructions were built; others give you a look at the builders themselves.

The builders, who were extraordinary people, are the second reason why these ten constructions were chosen. Each builder did something that others said couldn't be done. Each ran into trouble — not only from the doubters but from the huge problems of the tasks he tackled. All of the builders were people who thrived on the challenge of doing unbelievable things. All have a most important quality: fearlessness. Most people are afraid to try something that has never been done. The builders in this book overcame their own fears and the fears of those people who tried to stop them. They seem to have had endless imagination, too. Maybe this imagination was the key that unlocked other people from their fears and even inspired them to join the projects.

In spite of all the opposition these notable builders faced, they kept at their tasks. For instance, the Washington National Monument Society ran out of money many times, yet they continued building for more than a quarter of a century. Disease killed thousands of Panama Canal workers, but George Goethals did not quit. Even Edmund Wattis's death did not keep his dream of the Hoover Dam from coming true. In spite of heartbreaking discouragement, nothing could stop these people.

Though the builders were fearless, imaginative and unstoppable, none of their constructions would have been here today without many people working together. Just as an anthill is the work of hundreds of ants, every one of these beautiful, man-made constructions was built by people, for people. And they belong to the people—to you and me.

It has been said that seeing is believing, but millions of Americans who see these constructions still say, "That's incredible!"

1

Prehistoric High-Rise Apartments

The Cliff Dwellings

In 1960, deep inside a cave near Cortez, Colorado, an awesome discovery was made. It was the body of a baby girl who had been dead for seven hundred years. Covered and dry, her body was well preserved—even her hair. The mummy baby was wrapped in a blanket of feathers and buried beneath the floor of what was once her house.

The infant mummy was found in "Room 28" of a cliff dwelling called Long House. The room had been numbered by archaeologists making a dig for the National Geographic Society. Long House, one of many cliff dwellings discovered and studied during the past hundred years, is a kind of high-rise apartment building that was constructed centuries before there was a United States. Hundreds like it were built in caves high inside the walls of cliffs in an area called Four Corners, where Colorado, New Mexico, Arizona, and Utah meet.

Some of these cliff houses are five stories high and were built entirely within vast caves in the sides of the cliffs. The mummy baby was found in the Mesa Verde cliff dwellings. Mesa Verde is a flat-topped mountain. Its sides drop nearly straight down into canyons that are from one thousand to two thousand feet deep.

Cliff dwellings were thriving communities two hundred years before Christopher Columbus set foot in America. One of them was the tallest

Built: sometime during thirteenth century
Workers: anywhere from 25 to 300 people, depending on size of dwelling
Construction deaths: no figures available
Cost: no information available

3

United States Department of the Interior, National Park Service

apartment building in the United States up until a hundred years ago. In these massive constructions of stone and cement, early Native Americans showed themselves to be highly skilled craftspeople.

Mesa Verde's cliff dwellings were built by the Anasazi, ancestors of the modern Pueblo Indians. There are no true Anasazi left. They were a people who appeared, grew strong and then passed away into history.

Anasazi is a Pueblo word that means "old ones." The Anasazi were descendants of the first people in America. The best evidence says those first Americans came here from Asia fifteen thousand to forty thousand years ago. They probably crossed over a land bridge that once joined what are now the USSR and Alaska. These original immigrants migrated slowly down across North, Central and South America.

About two thousand years ago the Anasazi settled in what is now southwestern Colorado. At first they found shelter in caves, hunting plants and animals for food. By A.D. 500 they had learned to grow corn, beans and squash. They built more permanent homes in the caves.

After A.D. 500 the Anasazi moved from their caves to the top of Mesa Verde, an area of about three hundred square miles. There they built houses

Above: a section of Long House, the Mesa Verde cliff dwelling where the mummy baby lived with her family two centuries before Columbus discovered America.

Opposite: Long House was built in the 14th century and is the second largest cliff dwelling in Mesa Verde.

United States Department of the Interior, National Park Service

and grew crops. Their houses were pit houses; a wood pole frame was built over a shallow pit and covered with brush and adobe mud.

The Anasazi families lived closely together, sometimes even attaching their houses. Dogs roamed the courtyards, and flocks of wild turkeys were kept for food and feathers. In the fields around their houses, the Anasazi cultivated their crops. Thus had the mummy baby's ancestors lived for a dozen generations before she was born.

Around 1200 the Anasazi moved down from the mesa top into the deep caves that water had carved out of the cliffs over a long period of time.

National Archives

The cliff dwellings were built under ledges or in vast caves high above the canyon floors.

The Anasazi cut bricks from the sandstone cliffs and plastered them together with clay cement. Though their stone cutting tools were primitive, their technique was skillful, giving the walls of their dwellings a smooth, finished look.

Perhaps they moved because they needed more room for growing their crops on the mesa. Or perhaps enemy raiders forced them down underneath for protection. Inside the caves they built pit houses that were hidden high above the canyon floors, safe from enemies.

It was in these caves that their house building reached incredible heights of construction. The skillful Anasazi cut building blocks from the sandstone cliffs and fit them together into walls that are still standing after almost eight hundred years. The stone blocks were cemented with soft clay mixed with gravel. Some of the walls were also plastered with this clay cement.

Anasazi women probably supervised the construction. As in some modern Pueblo families, Anasazi women were the leaders of their households. The houses belonged to them. A child became a member of its mother's family. The father of a family was somewhat of an outsider. When a young man married, he went to live with his wife in her house. The wife's parents then built the newlyweds a house adjoining theirs.

Cliff dwelling walls have stood so long because they are built of a sturdy material and are nearly perfectly balanced. Few modern buildings will be standing eight hundred years from now. The walls of the cliff houses were almost perfectly straight and the corners practically square. Plumb walls, or walls that are perfectly straight with square corners, are not so incredible nowadays, but the Anasazi built them without the advantages of metal tools. They succeeded with simple stone axes and amazing skill.

Cliff Palace is another Mesa Verde apartment complex four miles from the home of the mummy baby. Cliff Palace was one of the first cliff dwellings to be discovered by white settlers about a hundred years ago. The construction is much like Long House, but bigger. Over three hundred feet long and one hundred feet wide, it is the largest ever found. Even so, its four-story housetops are far below the ceiling of its cave.

Cliff Palace was once a thriving city with over four hundred people living in its apartments. Most rooms were about six feet by eight feet in size. Doorways were merely crawl spaces. A mother, father and their children would live in one tiny room. When the children married, usually between the ages of fourteen and sixteen, the bride's parents would add another room beside or on top of theirs. The boxy apartments piled up inside the cave as families grew.

The Anasazi left behind many human traces of their presence in the cliff dwellings. Fingerprints, footprints, elbowprints and kneeprints are visible all over and speak clearly of these ancient people. Often Anasazi painted their walls with meaningful designs and pictures. Here and there are tiny handprints of Anasazi children who couldn't keep from autographing the wet cement.

Daily life was rugged for the Anasazi. The climb up and down the cliff that housed their dwelling was torturous. Often the only way up was a zigzag line of toeholds chipped out of the steep stone walls. In winter the stony cold of their caves gave them arthritis and other bone ailments.

The harsh environment shortened their lives, and few lived past age forty. Fully half of them died as babies, just as the mummy baby had. Children must have been special in Anasazi life: dead infants were often buried beneath their houses so parents could keep them nearby.

Cliff Palace, built in the 13th century and discovered in 1888, is the largest cliff dwelling ever found. Since its discovery, archaeologists have studied its 220 rooms and kept careful records of their findings.

United States Department of The Interior, National Park Service

Timbers like this doorpost (right side of door) tell of the 13th-century drought which is thought to have forced the Anasazi to abandon their cliffside home.

Anasazi were seldom taller than five and a half feet. The study of Anasazi mummies has shown that they were attractive people. Their skin was reddish brown and their soft, black hair was usually wavy.

The Anasazi left their cliff houses sometime toward the end of the thirteenth century. Birds, bats and mice moved in where families had lived in peaceful closeness. Why did they leave? Archaeologists suggest they left because they may have been without the one thing all people need to survive — water.

Dating the tree rings in the roof beams of cliff houses, archaeologists have determined when the Anasazi began building their dwellings. Other tree rings tell of a severe drought that started in the Southwest in 1276. Streams dried up. Crops were scorched in the fields. The dry spell lasted twenty-four years. It drove the Anasazi out to find new sources of water, forcing them to begin a new life.

The Anasazi drifted south into the Rio Grande River Valley of New Mexico and Arizona. There they mingled with other Native Americans, especially the Pueblos. Brush grew up around the old cliff houses and hid them for centuries. The red, yellow and brown hues of the stone dwellings were sealed away like treasures, waiting to be discovered in another time.

2

Uncle Sam's Highway

The National Road

The roads are impassable —
Hardly jackassable;
I think those that travel 'em
Should turn out and gravel 'em.

So sang Indianians in the 1840s about the longest road in the United States. This road, called the National Road, was to reach from Cumberland, Maryland, to Vandalia, Illinois. Begun in 1806, it was the first road built by the United States government. When the road reached Indiana in 1827, however, it was barely passable.

Road construction does not seem particularly incredible today. Giant earth moving machines build roads using a system that looks as easy as laying a carpet. In the early 1800s, however, roads were built by hand. Workers dug with shovels, rooted out trees with axes and hauled rock in wheelbarrows. To set out to build a six-hundred-mile road was unheard of.

For the first two hundred years of white settlement along the Atlantic seacoast, the Appalachian Mountains kept people from moving westward. In 1783, when Americans won their independence from England, lands

Built: 1806–1852
Workers: about 10,000
Construction deaths: 0
Cost: about $7 million (or
* $80 million in 1983)*

across the mountain barrier were still in dispute. France and Spain had claimed them first, but England also claimed them. After winning independence the United States said the land should belong to Americans so that the nation could expand.

By 1800 five millon people crowded the thirteen states. Those in search of better lands and a new life began scaling the mountain wall into the wilderness beyond. Before long a million people lived in the West, and the United States government feared they might start a separate nation. A road was needed to hold the nation together.

As a surveyor and young officer, George Washington had seen the need for an east-west road long before the United States was created. In 1755, during the French and Indian wars, Washington went with British General Edward Braddock and his troops across the Appalachians to stop the French from settling along the Ohio River. At that time there was no road over the mountains, making it nearly impossible to transport army supplies. General Braddock's army had to hack its way through the dense mountain forest. They chopped a road northwest from Cumberland, Maryland, at the frustrating rate of only three miles a day. When Braddock's army finally met the French, they had already battled through one hundred miles of forest and mountain. Braddock's troops were defeated.

As commander of the American army in the Revolutionary War, General Washington saw again how important roads were. At Valley Forge, Pennsylvania, in the bitter winter of 1777–78, poor roads nearly cut off supplies for his starving troops. Washington also knew from American settlers in the West that they needed a road to bring armies to protect them as well as supplies to build their settlements.

In 1791 President George Washington warned the United States government that a road to the West was desperately needed. Without one the French or Spanish might easily take away western settlements in the Mississippi River Valley.

There was still no National Road when George Washington died in 1799. In 1803, after purchasing the Louisiana Territory from France, President Thomas Jefferson urged Congress to build the National Road. Like Washington, he warned that Americans in the West might unite with British Canada or Spanish Mexico.

Jefferson was a shrewd leader. During his presidency the country doubled in size. Yet his proposal for a National Road faced opposition in Congress. As the President pushed for a road bill, the Congress divided. One side favored building the road; the other was against it.

Those against the road argued that the federal Constitution did not

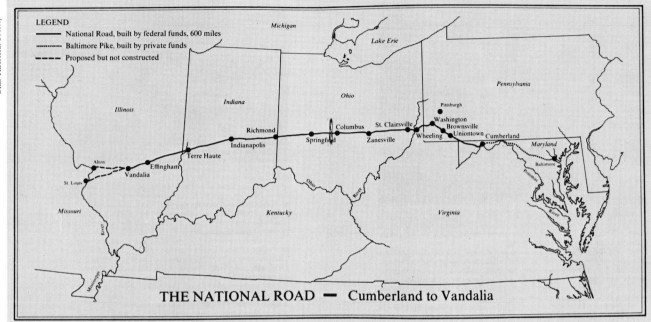

LEGEND
—— National Road, built by federal funds, 600 miles
········· Baltimore Pike, built by private funds
- - - Proposed but not constructed

THE NATIONAL ROAD — Cumberland to Vandalia

permit it. The road would benefit only part of the country, they said. The government should only pay for projects that would benefit all the states. Otherwise each state should build and pay for its own roads.

Congresspeople who favored the road insisted it would benefit the whole country. Americans, they said, would use the highway to settle the West. Farm products and other goods could be shipped on the road, helping to build and strengthen the nation. Besides, they argued, there were as yet no states along most of the roadway to pay for it.

Ohio settled the argument when it became a state in 1803. It was decided that Ohio land would be sold to settlers and 5 percent of the money would be used to build the road.

In 1806 Congress passed a National Road bill. President Jefferson boasted that Americans would soon go from Washington, D.C., to St. Louis, Missouri, in just six days. (It took from thirty to forty days at the time.) But Congress was not as enthusiastic. The bill provided just enough money to survey the road—and only as far as Ohio.

When the surveying was done, however, Congress acknowledged a growing demand for the road. Money was provided to begin construction in 1811. The road was to run some 130 miles, from Cumberland, Maryland, to Ohio's eastern border. The road itself would be twenty feet wide, with a

In 1852 the National Road connected five states from Maryland in the east to Illinois in the west.

five-foot shoulder on each side. The roadbed was to be paved with stone.

David Shriver, a construction engineer, was appointed superintendent of road construction. Shriver faced two huge problems: finding workers and building a safe, near-level road over steep mountains.

To solve the first problem Shriver put up posters in towns along the roadway advertising for engineers. Each engineer hired was to find local road workers and direct the building of a small part—about ten miles—of the road.

Workers were difficult to find. People who lived along the roadway were busy building their own homes and farms. About the only workers available were the Irish immigrants who had recently come to the United States. Most of them had left Ireland because of hard times there. They arrived in America eager to find work and make enough money to get settled. These people jumped at the chance to earn a living and were willing to move west with the road. If they were lucky, they might even be able to buy land in the Ohio River Valley.

The Irish road builders followed the road as it progressed slowly westward. They moved with their families, living in tents and shanties. Some of the

These farmers, hired to work on the National Road, were expected to supply their own horses and wagons.

workers settled along the road, their shantytowns later becoming villages like Donnelsville, Ohio, and Dublin, Indiana.

Some farmers were hired as roadworkers, too. They were experienced diggers, rooters and haulers. Because they had farms to look after, however, they couldn't go with the road crews as they moved farther west. They usually only worked a few weeks, then returned to their farms.

To build a near-level and safe road over the Appalachian Mountains was a far more difficult problem. David Shriver's survey had followed General Braddock's old road. Braddock's supply wagons had gotten over it, so most of it seemed safe, even for the loaded ten-thousand-pound Conestoga wagons that were expected to use the road. Still some parts of the mountains had to be dug out to make the road level. Many of the engineers were inexperienced, and parts of the road remained very steep. Over Mount Savage in Maryland, for example, the road rose over nine hundred feet for every linear mile. (Today a rise of more than four hundred feet per mile is considered unsafe.)

After the clearing and leveling came the problem of paving. In 1811 paving meant spreading broken rocks in layers over the roadway, twelve to

In 1827 the Fairview Inn fed and housed travelers along Maryland's section of the National Road.

National Archives

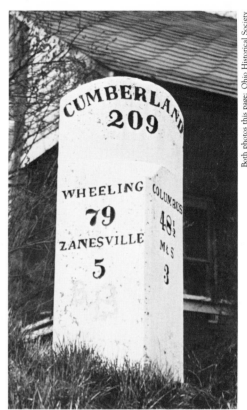

eighteen inches deep. Large rocks had to be broken into small pieces, and the Irish workers did most of the rock breaking. They sat on the ground and with one hand gripped the large rocks. With the other hand they swung a sledgehammer. Metal goggles with see-through slits protected their eyes from flying rock chips.

For the bottom layer of pavement, paving stones were supposed to be seven inches across. Inspectors checked them with seven-inch rings. Broken rocks had to pass through them; if they did not, they were broken again. The top layer required three-inch rocks. Sunup to sundown, through all kinds of weather, rock breakers smashed more than a half-million cubic yards of rock and spread them over the 128 miles of road. For this knuckle-breaking work they earned 25¢ a day. Farmers—who cut down trees and hauled dirt and rock—made 62½¢ a day. (The average laborer in the United States earned about $1 a day at that time.)

The first ten miles of the National Road took two years to build. Construction was haphazard, and much of the work had to be done over. After

Left: The western three-fourths of the National Road was little more than a trail in places like this, two miles west of Brownsville, Ohio.

Above: *this milestone was set up around 1830 on the National Road near Zanesville, Ohio.*

Rain and melting snow washed away much of the gravel "pavement" on this stretch of the National Road in Ohio. Photo taken around 1913.

seven long years the National Road was finished, ending at present-day Wheeling, West Virginia, on the eastern border of Ohio.

Long before it was completed, however, emigrants had begun using "The Road." By wagon they traveled at a rate of five miles an hour; by horseback they could speed up to ten. Up to two hundred thousand people a year traveled the road from 1810 to 1820. Toward the end of that decade, Americans were clamoring for the road to be built even farther west. In 1825 Congress finally agreed, and the road began to inch its way across Ohio.

US Highway 40 (right), as it looked in the early 1900s, alongside the old National Road route (left), near New Concord, Ohio.

For the next twenty-seven years, work on the National Road was sporadic. Sometimes Congress would provide additional money, but at other times anti-road members of Congress would stop it. In fact, most presidents after Thomas Jefferson opposed the road. John C. Calhoun, vice-president under Andrew Jackson, was one government leader, however, who fought to get the road built to St. Louis, Missouri. When arguments about the road flared in Congress around 1830, Calhoun cried out, "Let us conquer space!" For a time his determination helped get road construction moving again. Building the road in the nineteenth century was, in its way, as difficult as conquering outer space in the twentieth. Many continued to think the National Road was a waste of the nearly seven million dollars it eventually cost.

The western section of the National Road was not built as well as that first fourth, called the Cumberland Road. A few sections were paved with

Concrete pavement was first laid along this portion of the old National Road, west of Zanesville, Ohio, around 1912.

Ohio Historical Society

New meets old on the National Road, west of Hendrysberg, Ohio, as cars are forced to zigzag across an "S-bridge" around 1930.

oversize rocks and even logs. In some places tree stumps stuck up in the middle of the road. Bumps shook up travelers and even tore wheels off their wagons.

Funds for the National Road were finally cut off by congressional opponents in 1852. All work was stopped, partly because the Cumberland Road in the eastern section had been torn apart by forty years of emigrant traffic. Wagons had cut deep gouges in the road and made it nearly useless. Additional money for repair was out of the question.

By then, however, the road had done its job. Reaching to Vandalia, Illinois, seventy miles short of St. Louis, Americans could travel from Washington, D.C., to St. Louis in about ten days. About 10 percent of America's twenty-three million people had moved west along it. The road helped keep the West connected with the East and held the country together.

Even before work on the National Road was halted, trains were drawing travelers away from it. By 1842 the Baltimore and Ohio Railroad reached from Baltimore to Cumberland, Maryland. In 1853 it stretched to Ohio. Only people who couldn't afford train fare still used the National Road.

It took the automobile to renew Americans' interest in road building. During the 1900s thousands of automobilers were demanding more and more roads. In 1912 twenty-four miles of the National Road west of Zanesville, Ohio, were paved with concrete.

By 1923 some of the new Tin Lizzies were racing along at fifty miles an hour on a patchwork of dirt, brick, concrete and asphalt. An increasing number of accidents, plus the demand for more and better roads, put Uncle Sam back into the road-building business. By 1938 the National Road had been rebuilt and extended from the Atlantic to the Pacific oceans. It was renamed US Highway 40.

You may have traveled on the National Road without knowing it if you've ridden on US Highway 40 between Cumberland, Maryland, and Vandalia, Illinois. Today's Interstate 70 runs parallel to the old National Road. In some places, such as in eastern Ohio, Interstate 70 is the same road as US Highway 40 and the National Road.

The National Road was the first real interstate highway in America. During the first half of the nineteenth century, more than two million Americans traveled it to the West. Poet James Whitcomb Riley, who was born in 1849 along the National Road in Indiana, called it "the main artery of the whole living world." Riley may have exaggerated, but the people who were the lifeblood of the young American nation passed along that highway and kept the nation united.

3

A Fight
to the Finish

The Washington Monument

Built: 1848–1884
Workers: about 500
Construction deaths: 0
*Cost: about $1 million (or
 $13 million in 1983)*

Building a monument to George Washington does not seem so incredible; more than two hundred memorials have been named after him. Those in the United States include 1 state, 7 mountains, 8 streams, 9 colleges, 10 lakes, 33 counties, 121 towns and the capital city. Countless statues of Washington stand all over our country, as well as in London, Paris, Rio de Janeiro, Caracas, Tokyo and Budapest. The portrait on the American dollar bill may be the most famous face in the world.

George Washington was said to be first in war, first in peace and first in the hearts of his countrymen. Yet in the building of the Washington Monument, he proved to be last in their pocketbooks. It took a hundred years for Americans to dedicate a national monument to him.

In 1783 the Continental Congress made a unanimous decision to build a monument to Washington. Nothing further was done, however, until Washington died in 1799. United States Congressman John Marshall interrupted Washington's funeral to remind the American people of this sixteen-year-old unkept promise. He suggested a memorial grave for the first president beneath the Capitol Rotunda. But no one acted on Marshall's—or anyone else's—proposal for the next thirty years.

21

Meanwhile Washington's relatives could not agree on a place to bury him. His wife, Martha, agreed at first to bury him in Washington, D.C., but Washington's brother, John Augustine Washington, insisted he be buried at Mount Vernon, Virginia, Washington's home. So did Washington's adopted son, George Washington Parke Custis. Martha finally gave in to them, and that is where America's first president is buried.

By 1833 Americans who were weary of Congress's delay on a monument to Washington formed the Washington National Monument Society. John Marshall, who was by then Chief Justice of the United States Supreme Court, was elected president of the society. The society would do what the government could not, or so they thought. As it turned out, they quarreled more than Congress had.

Three years later the society had raised $28,000; not enough to build the monument, but enough for a contest to choose the best design. Architect

National Archives

The foundation for the Washington Monument was built around 1850, then later enlarged, as shown here, in the 1870s.

Robert Mills won with his model of a six-hundred-foot, four-sided tower that tapered to a pyramidal top. The base of this obelisk was a huge temple of Roman design. The society ignored the temple but began raising money for the tower. They estimated its cost at one million dollars.

Three well-known women were appointed to raise the money. They were Dolly Madison and Louisa Quincy Adams, former presidents' wives, and Mrs. Alexander Hamilton, wife of the former treasury secretary. They found their job impossible. In 1837 the country was in a financial slump; people had very little money to give. Congress was not willing to give money, either. At that time one million dollars was over a hundred times what a person could earn in a lifetime.

Ten years later the society had succeeded in collecting $87,000, which was enough to start construction. On the Fourth of July, 1848, the monument's cornerstone was laid. The stone was over thirty-six feet high and weighed 24,500 pounds. It had been hollowed out so that tokens of Washington's times could be placed inside. These included a 1783 penny, a United States flag, a Bible and newspaper clippings covering Washington's death.

Fifteen thousand people attended the cornerstone ceremony. Guests included Washington's son, President James K. Polk and other government officials—among them little-known Congressman Abraham Lincoln—state representatives and many Native Americans. There were speeches, prayers and fireworks—even some unexpected "fireworks" when people fought over chips of the marble cornerstone that were given away as souvenirs.

The society hoped the cornerstone celebration would fire enthusiasm for the monument, helping them raise more money. Most Americans had seen drawings of the memorial and liked it. Again, however, the fund raisers were left empty-handed. Why? Probably because the country was still in an economic depression and remained so throughout the 1840s. Another reason might be that though the new generation wanted the monument, they did not want to be the ones to pay for it. It is not uncommon for people to feel this way.

From 1848 to 1854 the Washington National Monument Society managed to collect $300,000 and the first 152 feet of the 600-foot tower were built. Pure white marble covered an inside wall of granite. The marble blocks were about 2 feet high, 1½ feet thick, and varied in width from 1 to 3 feet. The marble and granite walls were 15 feet thick at the base. In 1855 Congress pledged $200,000 toward the monument so that the building

Stones for the Washington Monument are raised by this chain-and-pulley crane, pictured here on October 7, 1879.

could continue. Construction was going smoothly. Then that same year there was a strange turn of events.

A secret society had formed whose members were prejudiced against "foreigners" as well as Catholics and the Catholic Church. These people, who called themselves the American Party, set out to destroy the monument because foreign countries and the Catholic Church had donated to it.

Through lying and trickery, the Know-Nothings, as other people called them, took control of the monument society in 1855. Over the next three years they raised a mere $285.09 and added four feet of construction to the tower. They used a poorer grade of marble, spoiling the appearance of the monument. The American people were outraged, and Congress withdrew its $200,000.

When the Know-Nothings were ousted and some of the original members of the monument society regained control in 1858, the cheap stone had to be removed. One fifty-foot pole-and-rope hoist was missing and another was broken. With inadequate equipment and no money, construction stopped. It had been seventy-five years since the idea of the monument was born, and only one-fourth of it was finished. For the next twenty-one years, no further work was done.

Part of the reason for this new delay was the Civil War. In those dark years cows, sheep and pigs—raised to feed the Union Army troops—grazed at the foot of the monument. Author Mark Twain saw the jagged obelisk and called it "a factory chimney with the top broken off." After the war ended in 1865, the monument society had even greater difficulty collecting money.

In 1876, during the nation's hundredth anniversary, the society gave the job of building the monument back to the United States government. Congress, in a patriotic mood, again voted $200,000 to finish the construction. A completion date was set for October 19, 1881, one hundred years after General Cornwallis surrendered to General Washington in the Revolutionary War.

The squabbling was far from over, however. People now argued that the monument should be modernized. They claimed the old foundation

Library of Congress

The monument looked, as Mark Twain once said, like "a factory chimney with the top broken off" during the Civil War.

TOP OF THE WASHINGTON MONUMENT.

SETTING THE CAPSTONE.

The Washington Monument capstone was set in place in 1884, as shown in this engraving.

Opposite: *Bird's-eye view of the Washington Monument, the Potomac River (foreground) and the United States Capitol Building (right, center) is captured in this Currier and Ives print from 1892.*

wouldn't hold up the six-hundred-foot tower. So the Army Corps of Engineers widened and deepened the foundation. It now runs fifty-seven feet below the tower floor and is solid enough to enable the tower to withstand 145-mile-an-hour winds.

Other people fought to make the tower shorter so that it would be more stable. This argument ended when the United States ambassador to Italy learned that the proper dimensions of an obelisk called for its height to be ten times its width. Since it was 55 feet wide, the height was cut from 600 to 555 feet.

One final construction problem left its mark on the monument itself. When construction resumed in 1879, engineers had trouble matching new marble with the old on the outside. They found and used marble that looked the same shade as the older marble. Years later the upper marble began to darken. That's why there's a ring around the Washington Monument, 152 feet up, to this day.

The 1881 deadline was long past when in December, 1884, the capstone was finally placed on the monument. It had a notch five inches wide at the top. This was to hold in place the nine-inch-high aluminum tip of the tower. It was the largest piece of aluminum ever cast, weighing one hundred ounces. On December 6, 1884, six officials climbed to the top to set the aluminum point in place.

With flags flapping in high winds, guns saluting and the crowd's shouts blown away on the wind, the monument was completed. Dedicated on Washington's birthday in 1885, the monument did not open to the public until 1888 because of unfinished interior work. The government had paid three-fourths of the total $1,187,710.31 it had cost.

Some twenty-three thousand stones were cemented together to make the monument. Weighing about 150 million pounds, it sways ever so slightly in a strong wind. At noon in summer, when the sun heats the south face, the

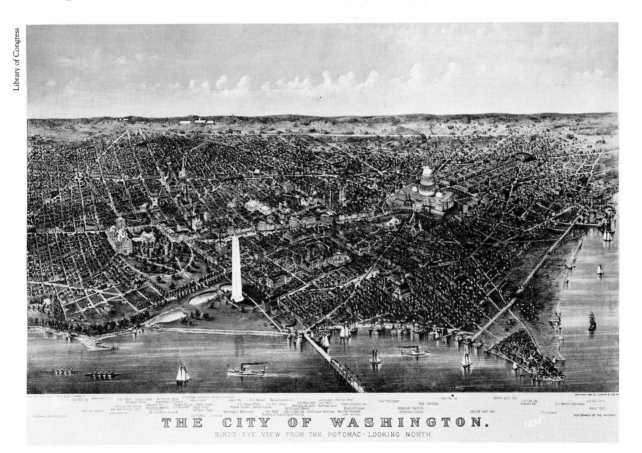

THE CITY OF WASHINGTON.
BIRDS-EYE VIEW FROM THE POTOMAC - LOOKING NORTH.

The Washington Monument in 1978 with a program in progress at nearby Sylvan Theatre.

stone expands and bends the tip of the monument northward a few hundredths of an inch.

From windows at the top of the tower, visitors—one and a half million every year—can see the White House, the Capitol Building, the Potomac River and Arlington Cemetery. On the granite blocks that line the inside, they can read the inscriptions of those who donated stones. The state of Virginia's stone, given around 1850, says: "Virginia Who Gave Washington to America Gives this Granite." For more than half a century after it was built, the Washington Monument was the tallest stone structure in the world. Today it ranks second. (The tallest is the tower commemorating the battle of San Jacinto, near Houston, Texas, at 570 feet.)

At the cornerstone-laying ceremony on July 4, 1848, Robert C. Winthrop, Speaker of the United States House of Representatives, prolonged the ceremony in the hot summer sun. Winthrop ended his ninety-minute speech by saying that in the future people everywhere would prolong the fame of George Washington. Ironically, people had certainly prolonged the building of a monument to him.

4

Ms. Liberty

The Statue of Liberty

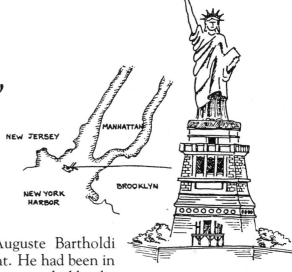

Built: 1875–1886
Workers: about 250
Construction deaths: 0
Cost: about $700 thousand (or
$6.5 million in 1983)

French sculptor Auguste Bartholdi fussed and fumed as he paced the deck of the elegant yacht. He had been in New York two days and still was not able to see his own statue, hidden by the thick fog that blanketed the harbor. It had taken Bartholdi eleven years to build this statue. Finally, in 1886, it stood completed in New York's harbor and he couldn't even see it.

"Auguste," said his wealthy American friend Richard Butler, "your statue is there, just as you created it. Come below and have some coffee. Maybe the fog will lift in a while." Bartholdi reluctantly followed his friend.

Bartholdi's wife, however, stayed up on deck. Suddenly the fog lifted and the Statue of Liberty her husband had created gleamed copper-bright in the sun. A huge French flag covered the face, and Bartholdi's wife stood spellbound by the sight.

Remembering Auguste, she called down for him to hurry and see his statue.

Bartholdi and Butler came on deck, but before they could get there, the fog had curtained off Miss Liberty again.

Auguste Bartholdi did not see his statue until the next day, October 28, 1886. That day, called Bartholdi Day, was the day of the unveiling.

New York had a big celebration. Schools let out and stores closed. Bands played, soldiers paraded, guns boomed — and rain drizzled down. Despite the weather a million cheering people turned out to salute the three-hundred-foot statue. *The New York Times* called it the day "a hundred Fourths of July broke loose."

Miss Liberty towered above tiny Bedloe's Island. In 1886 her height was fantastic — higher than any building in New York. The copper lady stood 151 feet from her toes to the tip of her torch, and she was on a pedestal that doubled her height. The "lady with the lamp" was the tallest sculpture in the world.

There was more to Miss Liberty than her unbelievable size. She was built in France, and the fact that she finally arrived in New York is a story in itself. The French, who paid for her construction, ran out of money many times. The Americans, to whom the statue was a gift, did not even want her — at first.

France had been close allies with this country since before it was the United States. The French had helped the Americans win their freedom from England in the War of Independence. Then, in 1789, the French staged their own revolution but failed to gain as much freedom as the Americans had. When Frédéric-Auguste Bartholdi was born in 1834, the French government was unstable. Napoleon I, emperor of France, ambitiously hoped to conquer Europe; the threat of war was constant.

Growing up in France, Bartholdi longed for the same liberties that Americans enjoyed. By the time he was eighteen, he had developed a love for sculpting and had his own studio. His first assignment was a statue of Jean Rapp, a French army general and a fighter for liberty.

Bartholdi made one mistake on this first job. The twenty-six-foot statue was too high for the door of the Paris salon where it was to be exhibited. The French people laughed; Auguste nearly cried. Making the best of the situation, he set up his statue outside and, because of publicity over his mistake, people flocked to see it. Those who had laughed before now praised Bartholdi's work. He received many new assignments. Auguste, who loved bigness, next sculpted a lion that was seventy-one feet long.

In the 1850s France enetered a period of great prosperity. Most of the money, however, was in the hands of a few people. The wealthy controlled the French government and denied many freedoms to the poor. Bartholdi and others opposed its policies and longed for more freedom in France. One of the others was Edouard Laboulaye, who had been a lawyer and teacher of great influence.

Bartholdi met Laboulaye at a dinner in 1865. They became friends, and Laboulaye told Bartholdi about the democratic government he and others hoped to bring about in France. It was to be called the Third Republic. He also discussed another idea he had that he hoped would help bring democracy to France.

France, said Laboulaye, could give the United States a monument to human liberty. The gift would help gain American support for the Third Republic. To Bartholdi this seemed a golden opportunity, a big idea that demanded a big statue. That night, the Statue of Liberty was born.

In 1870 France was at war with Germany, and the French government was tottering. The Third Republic was about to take over. Laboulaye and his group, in an effort to further their cause, sent Bartholdi to the United States to find out if Americans were interested in building a statue as a joint project. Laboulaye had many American friends and arranged for Bartholdi to meet some of them.

Bartholdi arrived in New York in June, 1871. While he was there, he decided that New York Harbor was the perfect place for his statue because immigrants were arriving there by boat every day.

President Ulysses S. Grant was one of the people Bartholdi told about his statue and the French idea of a joint project. Bartholdi wrote back to France that the president liked the idea. There is no record, however, that Grant mentioned the statue to anyone else. Bartholdi's English was poor, and he may have misunderstood much of what was said. In addition, Americans had just suffered through the Civil War; they were too hurt to build a statue with France.

Bartholdi returned to France that fall, insisting that Americans wanted the statue. With Laboulaye's approval, he set to work on a clay model. Laboulaye and others began raising money to pay for it.

By 1875 the Third Republic was in power and the influential Laboulaye had raised enough money to begin construction of the statue. Bartholdi excitedly gathered twenty craftspeople and showed them his forty-nine-inch model. He had sculpted a full-robed woman, long the symbol of liberty, who had the face of Bartholdi's mother and the body of his wife.

Neither stone nor bronze would do for the statue, the sculptor told his workers. They were too heavy and too expensive. Copper, he said, was just right. They set to work ambitiously.

First, three carefully measured enlargements of Bartholdi's model were sculpted in plaster. Each was several times larger than the one before. The third was full-sized, 151 feet high. It was built in pieces: the head, the right arm, the torso and so on.

Wooden forms were then built around each piece of the carefully crafted plaster model, conforming to its shape. The copper was hammered over the wooden forms, shaping it like the model beneath it. Many sheets of copper

United States Department of the Interior, National Park Service

The full-size model of the statue's left arm and tablet was under construction in the late 1870s.

United States Department of the Interior, National Park Service

Copper clothing for Miss Liberty was shaped in wooden forms, which had been built around each piece of the full-size model.

were used for each statue piece. The sheets were less than an eighth of an inch thick and easily bent.

After that thick lead was pressed against the plaster model, so that every crease and wrinkle was copied exactly. The plaster model was then removed, and the partly shaped copper sheets were gently hammered against the lead mold to give them their final form. The sheets could then be connected with rivets.

The copper form needed a frame to hold it up. Bartholdi hired Gustave Eiffel—who later built the Eiffel Tower—to build a skeleton. The skeleton was made of steel beams and had two thousand iron straps attached, to which the copper sheeting would be riveted. Eiffel built it to endure New York Harbor's gale winds and salty spray.

The statue was not finished, as Bartholdi had hoped, in time for the United States Centennial in 1876. The hand holding the torch had been completed, however, and Bartholdi took it to Philadelphia, Pennsylvania, for the International Centennial Exposition. Visitors were allowed to climb up into the torch, and the exhibition kindled American interest in the statue. Some joined in an effort to raise money to build the base on which it would stand.

Miss Liberty was completed in France in June, 1884. A year later the statue arrived in New York Harbor aboard the *Isere* in more than two hundred wooden crates. Her pedestal, however, was not ready to receive her. Americans had raised $200,000; they needed $100,000 more to complete the base. Construction had stopped. Then came Joseph Pulitzer. Through his New York newspaper, *The World*, he published a series of articles that shamed Americans into giving money. By August, 1885, the final $100,000 had been collected. Eighty percent of it was pennies, nickels, dimes and quarters from the poor.

The statue had cost France $400,000; Americans paid $300,000 for the base. The United States Congress gave $56,000 for the unveiling ceremony in 1886, which began with a three-and-a-half-hour parade that ended at the tip of Manhattan Island. The thousands who gathered there could not see Miss Liberty in the fog and rain, a mile and a half away on Bedloe's Island.

More than three hundred boats were in New York Harbor to take in the ceremony. One of the ships was a steamer rented by the Woman Suffrage Association. Ironically, its loudspeaker blared through the honking, tooting and whistling: "If the Statue of Liberty came to life, she would not be allowed to vote in the United States or France!" The Nineteenth Amendment, ratified in 1920, was later to guarantee that freedom.

An 1886 engraving shows Miss Liberty under construction atop the pedestal building.

United States Department of the Interior, National Park Service

Wooden forms were used to mold the 27,000-ton concrete and steel pedestal for the Statue of Liberty, shown here in 1885.

When the din died down and the unveiling ceremony was over, President Grover Cleveland told Bartholdi, "You are the greatest man in America today!"

By the time Bartholdi had returned to France, hundreds of visitors were climbing the spiral stairway to the top of his statue. The Statue of Liberty—his greatest achievement—would last forever, he said. Around 1900 Bartholdi learned that he had cancer. Though he was sick, he remained cheery. He even sculpted his own tombstone. Then, in 1904, he died.

Three years before Miss Liberty's unveiling, a young woman was asked to write a poem for the statue's pedestal. Her name was Emma Lazarus, and she was a champion of immigrant rights. Her poem is inscribed on the statue, and its last lines read:

> *Give me your tired, your poor,*
> *Your huddled masses yearning to breathe free,*
> *The wretched refuse of your teeming shore.*
> *Send these, the homeless, tempest-tost to me,*
> *I lift my lamp beside the golden door.*

To the millions of immigrants who passed by in the decades following

United States Department of the Interior, National Park Service

The Statue of Liberty stands on Bedloe's Island and faces New York's busy harbor.

1886, the Statue of Liberty came to mean *freedom* and *America*. Few remember that the Statue was French. Today two million people a year visit Miss Liberty, though they may only climb to her crown. The torch arm and other parts of the statue are in need of repair.

A federal advisory commission—with Bob Hope among its members—was established in 1982 to raise money to renovate Miss Liberty for her hundredth anniversary in 1986. If Americans will contribute to the statue's upkeep, her torch arm will be reopened and her future assured.

5

The Big Ditch

The Panama Canal

Parrots screeched and monkeys chattered, bright-colored flowers bobbed in a gentle breeze and pelicans on posts eyed the first ship to sail the Panama Canal on opening day, August 15, 1914. The weather was hot and muggy, as usual. Though rain threatened, spectators picnicked along the canal route, waving at the ship.

Built: 1904–1914
Workers: about 50,000
Construction deaths: 5,600
Cost: about $352 million (or
$3.5 billion in 1983)

Aboard the *Ancon*, a band struck up "The Star-Spangled Banner" as the ship entered the first series of locks. Passengers cheered and waved American flags. The *Ancon* carried many important officials who had helped build this "path between the seas." The most important person wasn't on the ship, however. George Goethals, the last of three chief engineers of the canal, chose to ride the rails beside the canal in a bright yellow railroad car.

The dream of a waterway across the Isthmus of Panama was an old one. It began with Columbus in 1502. He had explored the isthmus while searching for an all-water route around the world. For the next four centuries the idea of building a canal across this strip of land was discussed many times in many countries. A water highway connecting the Atlantic and Pacific oceans at this point would save weeks of ocean travel around the tip of South America. The owner of the connecting canal would have tremendous control over world trade.

Spain once owned the isthmus but lost control of it in 1822. That part of Central America became New Granada, as present-day Colombia and Panama were once called. The government of New Granada asked the United States to build a canal, and both France and England had already made surveys for a canal route there, but no one built a canal at that time. The United States had built a railroad across the isthmus by 1855, to carry people who were on their way to the gold rush in California. Nothing else was done for almost twenty-five years.

France was the first country to actually try to build the canal. In 1878 the French began the task of digging miles of channel, joining rivers and lakes

Library of Congress

President Theodore Roosevelt (center) visits the construction site of the Panama Canal in 1906.

and digging through a whole mountain near the town of Culebra. Disease defeated them, however. Tropical fevers raged in Panama's hot, wet jungles, and in ten years of construction, twenty thousand people died. In 1889 the French ran out of money. The canal was barely begun.

The United States finally recognized the need for a Panama canal when it became involved in the Spanish-American War of 1898. The American battleship *Oregon* was stationed in the Pacific Ocean and had to sail all the way around the tip of South America to get to Cuba, where the fighting took place. It took the *Oregon* nearly a month to reach the battle, which lasted only a hundred days. Fortunately the ship arrived in time, but obviously a way was needed to move ships from ocean to ocean more quickly.

Theodore Roosevelt had fought in the Spanish-American War. In 1903, after he became president, he urged the United States to build a Panama canal. Panama broke away from Colombia and became a republic in that year. Uncle Sam leased the land and purchased the French canal-building company. In 1904 Roosevelt ordered workers to "let the dirt fly!"

Before any dirt could fly, however, disease had to be conquered in this swampy land. Dr. William Gorgas, chief sanitary officer, was an expert in tropical diseases. Knowing that mosquitoes carry yellow fever and that these insects hatch from stagnant water, he began by draining ditches and puddles where mosquitoes bred.

Gorgas also made the four thousand canal workers drink quinine medicine at every meal. It had been known for three hundred years that quinine prevented and even cured malaria. Gorgas also screened windows to keep out the mosquitoes and fumigated wherever possible. In the first two years of construction, eighty-four workers died of yellow fever and malaria. After that Gorgas just about eliminated these diseases in Panama.

Though workers had called Gorgas a crank at first, the quiet, white-haired man was later revered. He became a medical hero of sorts and was highly respected by native Panamanians.

During Dr. Gorgas's crucial battle in Panama, Americans at home did not understand why the workers, nicknamed tropic tramps, weren't digging. Few people realized that before the digging could start, the tropic tramps had to rescue French machinery in the jungle and rebuild rotted buildings. The first chief engineer, John Wallace, was criticized. Americans, impatient for results, said Wallace wasn't forceful enough to build the canal. Wallace, who lived in mortal fear of disease and brought his own casket with him to Panama, quit his job in 1905 and returned home.

Next came fifty-two-year-old John Stevens as chief engineer. He was called Big Smoke Stevens because of his big cigars and forceful character. Before Stevens took the job, hundreds of workers had quit because they were afraid of disease. Stevens told the workers, "There are three diseases here: yellow fever, malaria and cold feet. The worst is cold feet." His humor and confidence won the workers over.

Big Smoke Stevens did not begin digging right away, either. Instead he spent money providing better housing and food for his seventeen thousand workers. A huge department store was built so that canal employees could buy almost anything they needed. They were given better recreation facilities, too.

Before he was chief engineer on the Panama Canal, Stevens had been a railroad builder. One of the greatest feats of his entire career was rebuilding the rundown railroad in Panama that carried away dug-up dirt and rock, called "spoil." By late 1906 Steven's trains had hauled over a half-million cubic yards of spoil out of the cut at Culebra.

When Stevens began digging this cut through the mountains in 1906, he realized the Culebra Cut was going to be the most demanding part of the canal construction. It was to be some 350 feet deep and eight miles long. When the digging finally began, twenty-five steam shovels, weighing ninety-five tons apiece, dug away at Culebra. Knowing the cut would take about seven years, Stevens announced that the canal would open by January 1, 1915.

Canal diggers called Culebra Hell's Gorge. Daytime temperatures reached 130 degrees, and as the workers dug, greasy, soapy clay kept sliding down the sides of the giant V to fill the dug-out spaces. Clay and rock were squeezed up out of the bottom. Endless dirt slides eventually forced diggers to widen the cut to three times its planned width.

Big Smoke Stevens then faced one of the biggest decisions of the canal project. Should the whole canal be dug to sea level? Or should it have locks to lift ships over the mountains?

Without locks the canal would have to be dug very deep and narrow and would be dangerously twisty. Locks, though they were a better idea, would be very expensive. Much more money would be needed.

Stevens returned to the States in 1906 to convince Congress to put up more money. Reluctantly Congress agreed, and that fall Teddy Roosevelt himself visited the canal construction site.

Then suddenly, in April, 1907, John Stevens resigned. He never explained why. Was he tired of eighteen-hour workdays? Or was he weary of fighting for money and supplies? Some claimed he quit in anger on the spur of the moment.

Stevens's replacement was a person he had once refused to hire as his assistant, George Washington Goethals. The six-foot Goethals had visited the canal site in 1905 and declared the job hopeless. He changed his mind in 1907, however, when he saw all that Stevens had accomplished.

President Roosevelt, weary of replacing his chief engineers, wanted someone who would finish the canal. Colonel Goethals was an army officer

Opposite, above: *trains are used to haul spoil from Culebra Cut in 1904.*

Below: *canal workers gently push dynamite sticks with poles deep inside holes to blast away the rock and earth at Culebra Cut. Photo taken in 1912.*

Dirt and rock slides made Culebra Cut a never-ending digging task. This steam shovel was buried by a slide in February, 1913.

and would not be able to quit. Roosevelt, giving him more power than Wallace or Stevens, appointed Goethals chairman of the Panama Canal Commission.

Goethals was as skilled in canal construction as Stevens was in organizing the job. Stevens had made a good start and had planned well enough for the canal to be opened on time. There were now thirty thousand workers. Goethals, less flashy than Big Smoke Stevens, worked his crews harder and longer, but he treated people fairly and workers respected him.

Since Dr. Gorgas had quieted the fear of disease, it became easier to get workers. Goethals soon expanded the work force to forty thousand. Many had come from as far away as Spain, Greece and Italy. Goethals also hired Jamaican and Irish laborers as well as Sikhs from India.

Colonel Goethals faced three huge tasks in Panama: cutting through Culebra, damming the Chagres River and building the canal locks. The Culebra Cut was only one-fourth finished, and Goethals would soon be excavating a million cubic yards a month there.

To tame the wild Chagres River, Goethals decided to build Gatun Dam. This earth dam would be built from the Culebra spoil. It was the biggest dam ever built — 23 million cubic yards. (Today the Tarbela Dam in West Pakistan holds the record — 186 million cubic yards.) Gatun Dam was designed to create Gatun Lake, which would be the source of the water to operate the locks.

The locks, Goethals's third task, were built of concrete and steel. Each lock is as long and high as a five-block row of six-story buildings. The three pairs of Gatun Locks, at the Atlantic end of the canal, raise or lower a ship eight-five feet. In doing so they use enough water from Gatun Lake to supply a major city for an entire day.

At the Pacific end of the canal are the Pedro Miguel and Miraflores locks. Together they raise or lower ships about eighty feet. The slightly larger Miraflores Locks are the world's largest lock system. All together the Panama locks are the greatest construction feat in canal history, with six pairs of locks in all.

On May 20, 1913, shovels from both ends of the Culebra Cut broke through and met. At Gatun Lake a thin wall of earth held back the waters that would fill the canal. Dynamite was now planted along this last barrier. Its wires were hooked up to receive a telegraph signal from the White House in Washington, D.C.

At 2:00 P.M. on October 10, 1913, President Woodrow Wilson pushed a button in Washington. In Panama, two thousand miles away, an explosion

Damming the wild Chagres River was one of the biggest and riskiest jobs in building the Panama Canal. Photo taken in 1913.

released water into Culebra Cut. The locks at the Pacific end were still to be completed, but by the end of 1913 the waters of the Atlantic and Pacific oceans met.

The Panama Canal had been the largest and costliest construction project in history. Though its particular problems had all been solved before on other projects, the number and size of the construction tasks were mind boggling. For example, if all the spoil from the Panama Canal had been piled onto one city block, it would have reached nineteen miles in the air.

On the opening day, August 15, 1914, the *Ancon* sailed the canal from ocean to ocean, a distance of 50.72 miles, in about eight hours. The canal had cost Americans $352 million; the French, $287 million; making the total cost $639 million. The combined French and American construction on the canal had also cost some twenty-five thousand lives.

Today the Panama Canal carries over fifteen thousand ships per year, earning more than $140 million in tolls. Ship tolls are charged by the ton, and the average toll is about $10,000. In 1975 the *Queen Elizabeth II* paid the highest toll ever: $42,077.88. (Richard Halliburton was the first person

Library of Congress

This Panama Canal Lock could hold five city blocks full of six-story buildings. Its gates were still under construction when this photo was taken in 1913.

to swim the canal, in 1928, weighing 140 pounds. His toll was 36¢.)

The Panama Canal will not always belong to the United States. Our original lease with Panama was to expire in 2003. During the late 1970s, however, the United States agreed to turn parts of the canal over to Panamanians during the rest of this century. By the year 2000 the entire canal will belong to Panama.

On opening day, August 15, 1914, the S. S. Ancon, with flags flying, passes through the Pedro Miguel Locks of the Panama Canal.

6

Underwater Wonder

The Holland Tunnel

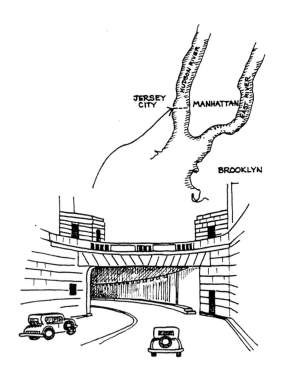

Built: 1920–1927
Workers: about 500
Construction deaths: 15
Cost: about $42 million (or
* $237 million in 1983)*

Just before the 1920s New York City had a headache of a traffic problem. Henry Ford's Model T had become a best seller, and New York's streets were clogged with Fords and many other cars. All vehicles going into or out of the city had to cross either the Harlem, the East or the Hudson river. The Hudson River was crossed by two million vehicles a year.

The only way to get over the rivers was by car ferries, which were slow and carried only a few cars at a time. Cars sometimes had to wait in line at the docks for hours. To solve this problem the people of New York and New Jersey decided to build a tunnel under the Hudson River. It would reach from Jersey City, New Jersey, to New York City, a distance of about a mile and a half.

In 1919 the tunnel commission was about to appoint George Goethals—one of the chief engineers of the Panama Canal—to build the tunnel. Goethals proposed to build a tunnel that would be forty-two feet wide. Another engineer, however, told the commission that Goethals's tunnel would not work because it was too wide.

This other engineer—slim, tanned, and thirty-six years old—had built four tunnels for subway trains under New York's East River. "Your tunnel is

The Port Authority of New York and New Jersey

Clifford M. Holland spent many twenty-four-hour days working on the tunnel that would be named after him. Photo taken in 1925.

too wide," Clifford Holland told the commissioners. "A forty-two-foot tunnel is too risky to build." He explained how each foot of tunnel width multiplies construction dangers many times. The science of tunneling was still very new, and Clifford Holland was concerned about the safety of tunnel workers.

"The tunnel should be no wider than twenty-nine feet," Holland warned them. Also, he said, its walls should be built of concrete and cast iron, not just concrete, as Goethals planned. Pressure beneath the riverbed would crush concrete.

The commissioners, convinced they were better off with Holland, appointed him chief engineer for the tunnel. It proved a wise choice, because all vehicle tunnels built since then have used Clifford Holland's methods.

At that time there were two methods for tunneling: the trench method and the shield method. In the trench method a trench is dredged from a construction barge floating on the river. The prefabricated tunnel is then floated out and sunk into the trench. Holland, however, chose the newer shield method. The shield is a hollow steel cylinder that protects workers while they dig out and construct the tunnel from under the river.

Imagine hammering a can, with no top or bottom, into a dirt bank. You scoop out the dirt that fills the can and hammer the can farther into the bank. A tunnel remains behind the can. This is somewhat like shield tunneling. The shield Holland used was thirty feet in diameter and sixteen

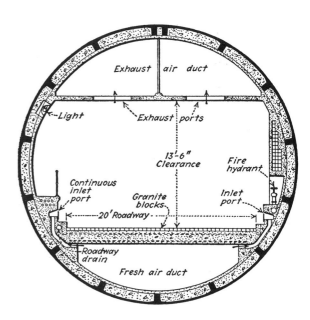

Above: *cross section showing one tube of the Holland Tunnel.*

Left: *after being driven into the ground beneath the Hudson River, a tunnel shield is ready to enter the caisson at the end of the south tunnel. Photo taken in 1924.*

feet long. Powerful jacks drove it forward as the dirt was shoveled out the rear of the shield.

To decide the height of the tunnel and the width of the roadway, Holland studied the proportions of cars and trucks. In 1920 cars were higher than they are today—six feet tall or more, compared with five feet or less today. Trucks in those days were no higher than our tallest trucks today— about twelve feet. So Holland decided that the inside of the tunnel should be thirteen feet high.

To decide on the tunnel's width, Holland considered that cars were about six feet wide, trucks were eight feet, and a team of three horses took up nine feet. He designed a roadway twenty feet wide, allowing for a passing lane. The tunnel would have two tubes, one for traffic running east and the other west. Each tube would have two lanes.

Tunnel construction began in 1920. First, hollow steel tubes, called *caissons*—from the French word meaning "box"—were driven down into the ground near the river, on both the Jersey and the New York sides. Each caisson was about thirty-five square and the same in height. The dirt was removed from the caissons, and a thirty-foot-diameter circle cut through the sides facing the river. Then four-hundred-ton tunneling shields were lowered by crane into the caissons and forced out through the side holes.

The shields began to bore their way toward the river, the front edges cutting like the rim of a can. Thirty powerful hydraulic jacks attached to the rear of each shield pushed against the caissons. They moved the shields forward two and one-half feet, and then the jacks were released. A cast-iron ring the same diameter as the shield was built between the shield and caisson. The jacks pushed against this ring, and the shield advanced several feet more.

Each time the shield moved, another iron ring was bolted to the one before. These rings, weighing eight tons apiece, formed the wall of the tunnel.

June 19, 1924: tunnel workers tighten bolts on cast-iron rings around the tubes.

9077

With each thrust of the shield, dirt flowed in through the front and had to be shoveled out. It was mostly mud, and the workers who shoveled it were called "sandhogs." As the tunnel grew, a track was laid along the bottom, and mining cars were used to carry the dirt back to the caisson to be removed.

The biggest problem Clifford Holland faced was keeping water out of the tunnel. It poured in with every forward shove of the shield. To keep the tunnel dry, a sixty-foot section right behind the shield was blocked off and made airtight. A ten-foot-thick concrete wall was built at the rear of this working section. Then air was pumped through tubes in this wall into the work chamber at low pressure. The air pressure held the water out.

Other air-lock tubes were built through the rear wall of the work chamber, allowing workers and dirt cars to come and go without letting the air escape. In the working section workers shoveled the dirt into the cars for removal, forced the shield forward and constructed the tunnel walls behind it. As the tunnel moved forward, the rear wall of concrete was rebuilt to keep the working section about sixty feet long.

While two shields were digging their way toward each other from opposite sides of the river, Clifford Holland was trying to solve the ventilation problem. He designed ventilator buildings for his tunnel with fans thirteen feet high that could blow fresh air through pipes into the tunnel floor. Other fans sucked exhaust fumes out through the ceiling.

Conducting ventilation experiments and overseeing the tunneling operations were each full-time jobs. Holland did both, often working twenty-four hours a day. After four years his health began to fail, and doctors warned him to rest. Finally he took a vacation. Pale and weary, he went to a hospital in Battle Creek, Michigan, to recuperate.

Then suddenly, on October 27, 1924, forty-two-year-old Holland died of heart failure in the hospital. Two days later the tunnels from each side of the Hudson "holed through." Sadly, the workers canceled celebration plans. Friends remembered Clifford Holland's words upon graduation from Harvard: "I am going into tunnel work, and I am going to put a lot more into it than I'll ever be paid for."

Though Holland had solved most of the design and construction problems, the tunnel was only half done. Milton Freeman took over as the new chief engineer, but five months later Freeman, also a hard worker, collapsed and died on the job. His heart, too, gave out. The next chief engineer was Ole Singstad, and it was he who finished the Holland Tunnel.

After the iron rings were in place, they had to be lined. A rectangular box of steel and concrete was built along the inside of both tunnel tubes,

Sandhogs shoveled the clay dirt by hand in this cross-passage dug between the tunnel tubes near the middle of the Hudson River. Photo taken in 1924.

forming the roadways. The rectangular box left spaces at the top and bottom of the surrounding tube for fresh air intake and exhaust outlet. The floor of the roadway was paved, and the walls and ceiling were tiled in white. Lights were hung along the walls.

Ole Singstad arranged for the completion of the four ventilation buildings, two on the New Jersey side and two in New York. Each building housed fans that ventilated one-fourth of the tunnel. The fans started up as opening day approached.

On November 13, 1927, cars and trucks wheeled into the new Holland Tunnel, named after the man who created it. Horns honked, announcing the first vehicles to make the underwater crossing. It cost $42 million to build the Holland Tunnel, which was fifty percent more than Holland had estimated. The tunnel took seven years to build. After Clifford Holland's success, other vehicle tunnels modeled after his design were built all over

Even with the speedy new tunnel, cars and trucks line up to cross the Hudson River on this day in July, 1931.

The Port Authority of New York and New Jersey

The Holland Tunnel, much as it looks today. Photo taken in July, 1935.

the world. The Holland Tunnel is 1.6 miles long; it was the longest of its time. (Today many underwater road tunnels are wider and longer. The longest is the Kanmon Tunnel in Japan, completed in 1958. It runs 6 miles, from Honshu to Kyushu.)

In the fall of 1983, to honor Clifford Holland's achievement, a plaque was placed at the Holland Tunnel entrance by the American Society of Civil Engineers. It proclaims the tunnel a historical engineering landmark.

7

Taming the Raging Red

The Hoover Dam

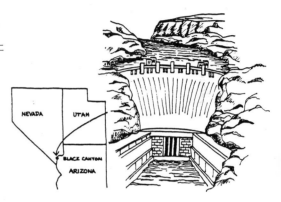

Built: 1931–1936
Workers: 5,250
Construction deaths: 96
Cost: about $165 million (or
  $1 billion in 1983)

For centuries the Colorado River was on the rampage, raging across the western half of the United States unchecked by any dam. The Raging Red, as the river has been called, can sweep up boulders weighing many tons and grind them to gravel and sand as the water rushes along. The river's current carries tremendous power, and until the Hoover Dam, nothing could tame it.

The Hoover Dam, begun in 1931 and completed in 1936, was built in Black Canyon, one of the deepest, narrowest canyons of the Colorado River. It is wedged between canyon walls that are 1,244 feet wide and 726 feet high. The dam resembles a concrete plug, weighing about seven million tons, and does three jobs: it controls the raging waters of the river, lets out water as needed for farmland and provides electricity.

The Hoover Dam was not the first dam to try to control the Colorado River. For years Americans had dreamed of taming the Raging Red, controlling its floods and using its water to irrigate the land.

Around 1900 the California Development Company tried to divert part of the Colorado River across the southern California desert by digging the Imperial Canal. They hoped the canal, with the help of smaller tributary canals, would irrigate the desert and turn it into rich farmland.

When the Colorado flowed through the Imperial Canal into the desert, the land blossomed. Ten thousand settlers flocked into what is now called the Imperial Valley. By 1904 farmers were harvesting wheat, alfalfa and melons from land that had been dry desert only a few years before.

The Raging Red was not to be tamed, however. In 1905 the river rose over its banks and flooded the Imperial Valley, tearing crops, houses and people out by their shallow roots. Though settlers replanted, the river was to flood many times over the next twenty-five years.

These troublesome floods caused George Chaffey, engineer of the Imperial Canal, to try to dam and channel the Colorado River at the southeast corner of California. He used dirt, wood, rocks—even sticks—to persuade the Raging Red to flow politely to farms in the Imperial Valley, but the river soon demolished his dam.

At about this time Arthur Davis, who worked for the United States Bureau of Reclamation, had an idea about how the Colorado River could help put the land to good use. His idea was simple: build a huge dam in one of the deepest canyons of the Colorado River, taming the river once and for all. Unfortunately, his idea was too big for its time. No one knew how to build a dam that big.

While Davis was pondering his idea, another person, Edmund Wattis, was learning about dam construction. Wattis had started out as a railroad worker and had worked on the first transcontinental railroad in the 1860s. In 1900 he had started his own construction company, which laid thousands of miles of railroad in the West. From his railroad experience he had built more than 250 tunnels as well as dams. Wattis was interested in building large dams, and each dam he built was larger than the one before.

By the 1920s Wattis's know-how was equal to the task of making Davis's idea a reality. When Congress decided to dam the Colorado, they chose Edmund Wattis to do it. Wattis formed a company made up of his own and five others, to handle the enormous job of building the dam. He called it Six Companies, Inc., and was later elected its president.

When Hoover Dam construction was about to begin, Wattis was in his seventies and his health was failing. He chose forty-nine-year-old Frank Crowe as chief engineer at the dam and Walker Young, of the US Bureau of Reclamation, as Crowe's co-engineer. They were a capable team.

The Hoover Dam was designed by Edmund Wattis. It was the first arch-gravity dam, so-called because it was arched into the current of the Colorado, making it stronger than a straight-across dam. The bottom of the dam is thicker than the top. It stands stoutly over a low center of gravity.

Opposite: *Hoover Dam was built in Black Canyon, one of the deepest, narrowest canyons of the Colorado River. Lake Mead was created behind the dam.*

United States Department of the Interior, Bureau of Reclamation

April 20, 1932: a high-wire surveyor, called a rigger-rodman, holds a rod on points which are recorded by surveying crews in the canyon below.

Crowe and Young had a lot to do before the dam could be started. The five thousand workers would have to have a place to live near the dam site, and an entire town had to be created. Black Canyon was twenty-five miles southeast of Las Vegas, in the Nevada desert. There were no towns nearby. Boulder City, Nevada, was the name of the town that was built on a site seven miles from the dam. It was higher and cooler than Black Canyon and had houses, a school and a church.

Construction of the dam started at the beginning of the Great Depression of the 1930s. The project gave jobs to thousands of people and paid them 50¢ to $1.25 an hour. These were good wages when millions of Americans were earning $1 a day or less. Job seekers flocked to Black Canyon.

Though lodging conditions at Boulder City were good, working conditions at the dam site were unhealthy. Besides the dangers of towering heights and working with heavy machines and explosives, the heat in the canyon was a threat to workers' lives. Summer temperatures averaged 120 degrees. Sixteen people died from heatstroke the first summer.

To protect the workers, dam officials brought in a medical expert from Harvard University. Dr. David Bruce Dill made an important discovery at Hoover Dam: people working in intense heat need more salt. Dr. Dill added table salt to the workers' drinking water, and the heatstroke deaths stopped.

In addition to Boulder City, workers built a roadroad and a highway to haul equipment and materials to and from the dam site. A concrete-mixing plant—the largest in the world—was set up nearby. A cableway with a crane suspended from it was hung across Black Canyon to lower materials to the bottom.

At last, in mid-1931, dam construction began. Two mammoth tunnels were blasted into the canyon walls on each side of the river. These tunnels were to channel the waters of the Colorado around the dam site, keeping the site dry during construction.

To carve these tunnels, monstrous machines, called "jumbos," drilled thirty holes at once. Some of the holes were as deep as twenty feet. Dynamite was set, and with a deafening roar the blasted rock fell to the tunnel floor. Each blast took an hour and a half and carved out seventeen feet of

United States Department of the Interior, Bureau of Reclamation

Dynamite blasts such as this one in July, 1931, echoed down Black Canyon daily during early construction.

tunnel. When the four tunnels were completed, they were lined with concrete. It took two and a half years to create the four 4,000-foot tunnels that were to divert the river around the dam foundation.

In June, 1933, the dam itself was started. Forms were built into which wet concrete was poured, creating the building blocks. Each of these concrete blocks was from twenty-five to sixty feet square and five to thirty feet high. Builders poured one and moved on to the next, until they had the bottom layer of blocks in place. Then they built another layer of blocks on top of the first, and then another. For almost two years they piled up the blocks to make the dam that would plug Black Canyon.

Engineers Crowe and Young had a problem drying the concrete. Chemicals in concrete give off lots of heat during the drying process. The more than three million cubic yards in the dam would take 150 years to cool and dry if Crowe and Young did nothing. To solve their problem they inserted small pipes into the wet concrete. Cold water was piped through the blocks to cool them, and the thousands of blocks dried in just twenty-two months.

Beginning of Hoover Dam construction in February, 1932, with bridge and bypass tunnels under construction.

Before the dam was finished Edmund Wattis, its creator, was on his deathbed in a hospital at Ogden, Utah. Frank Crowe built a model of the dam and wheeled it into Wattis's room. It was a perfect replica of the Hoover Dam. The old man's eyes lit up, and he smiled.

"It's your exact design, Mr. Wattis," whispered Crowe. "You're seeing the dam just as it will be."

Edmund Wattis died on February 3, 1934. The dam was completed on May 29, 1935. Engineers had said it couldn't be done, yet Crowe and Young had not only built it but had finished it two years ahead of schedule.

After the dam was finished, workers built a U-shaped powerhouse that covered ten acres. It was built at the downstream base of the dam. Seventeen generators were installed to turn the water power into electricity. Today the dam produces six billion kilowatt-hours of electricity a year, supplying countless cities and towns in Utah, Arizona, Nevada and Califor-

United States Department of the Interior, Bureau of Reclamation

The concrete blocks are piled up in Black Canyon as the dam nears completion in October, 1934.

nia with power. Money from selling this power has been paying for the dam since its completion.

The dam works this way: the Colorado River backs up against the dam, creating 115-mile-long Lake Mead behind it. Four intake towers feed water through pipes to turn the generators at the base of the dam. The generators turn water power into electric power.

Water not used by the intake towers goes into spillways on each side of the dam. It rushes through bypass tunnels and back into the river downstream. Some water from Lake Mead is piped out to Boulder City for drinking water.

During high-water times of spring and summer, the Hoover Dam prevents flooding along the lower Colorado. In dry weather the dam feeds water to farmlands, such as the fruitful Imperial Valley. Lake Mead also provides excellent fishing and boating, with 550 miles of shoreline.

When completed in 1936, Hoover Dam was the largest structure of any kind in the world. Though it had already begun some of its operations the year before, Hoover Dam was officially opened by President Franklin D. Roosevelt on December 11, 1936. All totaled, the dam cost $165 million.

Part of the dam's expense was for a new canal system to irrigate Imperial Valley and Coachella Valley in southern California. This system, over two hundred miles long, is called the All-American Canal and branches out from the Colorado River near the southeast corner of California. The Hoover Dam has ended for good the disastrous floods of eight decades ago in that reclaimed desert land.

The Hoover Dam not only stops the Colorado River from flooding downstream; it also stops silt. Silt is dirt and rock particles that the racing Colorado sweeps up along its course. When the Hoover Dam slows the river down, silt settles to the bottom of Lake Mead. The dam stops millions of tons of silt every year.

When the Hoover Dam was built, engineers estimated that silt would pile up to its crest in about three hundred years. Since then, however, another dam, called Glen Canyon Dam, has been built upstream. It collects 75 percent of Colorado River silt before it reaches Lake Mead. With this dam in place, the Raging Red should stay harnessed for at least four hundred years.

8

Mountain Carving

Mount Rushmore

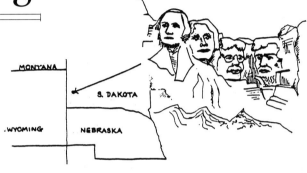

MONTANA

S. DAKOTA

WYOMING   NEBRASKA

Agiant is an ordinary person who is bigger than his world." Gutzon Borglum said this before he sculpted the Rushmore National Memorial in South Dakota, but he could easily have been referring to himself. His career as a sculptor was a giant achievement, not just because of his ambition but because of the sheer size of his creations. In 1941, when the four presidential faces on Mount Rushmore were completed, they were the largest sculptures in the world.

Long before Rushmore National Memorial was finished, thousands of visitors came to see it, and today over two million people a year come from all over the world. Except for the Golden Gate Bridge in San Francisco, California, Mount Rushmore is the most visited attraction in the United States.

The gigantic heads are sixty feet high. If they had bodies to match, George Washington, Thomas Jefferson, Theodore Roosevelt and Abraham Lincoln would be five stories tall.

It is more than their bigness, however, that inspires viewers. The four famous faces chiseled out of the granite mountain stir deep feelings in people. The presidents seem to come alive—as if they are about to speak.

Gutzon Borglum, the son of Danish immigrants, had already had some

Built: 1927–1941
Workers: 137
Construction deaths: 0
Cost: about $1 million (or $6.5 million in 1983)

61

mountain carving practice when he began the Rushmore project in 1927. Dozens of statues by the sculptor stood all over the United States, including twelve in our nation's capital, and he had sculpted others overseas, earning him worldwide fame.

The idea for Mount Rushmore came from Doane Robinson, a lawyer and state historian from South Dakota. In 1923 Robinson proposed a sculpture in the Black Hills. He suggested it be a memorial to heroes of the West, such as Lewis and Clark or Chief Red Cloud of the Sioux. Robinson had heard of Borglum's work, and in 1924 he wrote to the sculptor.

Borglum's greatest love was mammoth sculpture. Having grown up in the West and loving that part of the country, he went to South Dakota immediately. He brought his twelve-year-old son Lincoln and, with guides, they rode on horseback all over the Black Hills in search of a suitable mountain.

In 1925 Borglum chose Mount Rushmore in the Mount Harney Range. The sculptor also suggested to Robinson that the memorial should be not just to the West but to the whole country. Robinson agreed, and with other South Dakota businesspeople, he formed the Mount Harney Association. The association raised $54,000 and in 1927 hired Borglum to begin sculpting. Borglum was sixty years old when he began the project, which he expected to complete in five years. Presidents Washington, Jefferson, Roosevelt and Lincoln were chosen to symbolize American democracy, a theme Gutzon Borglum believed in wholeheartedly.

He began by building a clay model in a studio at the foot of Mount Rushmore. He scaled it so that one inch on the model was the same as one foot on the mountain. He also tackled the problem of getting workpeople up the sheer mountain face by building a stairway to the top. (There were 760 steps, which is about fifty times an average household stairway! In 1936 an aerial tramway was installed.)

To lower workers down the mountain Borglum used the "swing chair," an invention he had made at Stone Mountain. Leather straps attached a seat to a cable that was fixed at the top of each carved head. Cable cranks raised and lowered the chairs. Workers buckled straps around their waists so that even if they were knocked unconscious, they could not fall out.

Once the clay model was completed, Borglum faced the problem of how to transfer the face patterns from the model to the mountain. Sketching a sixty-foot head on the cliff would have been like drawing on paper while it is held up against your nose. Borglum devised "pointing," which works as follows. A small pivoting pole was bolted to the top of each clay model head; then a wire was hung from the pole down over the face.

Likewise, on the carved mountain heads, Borglum placed similar poles that were twelve times as long. A three-hundred-foot cable hung down over each face. If the tip of the clay model's nose was forty *inches* down the wire on the model, it would be forty *feet* down the cliff face. In this way the details of each face were marked on the mountain, resulting in nearly perfect proportions.

Once the faces were marked, holes were drilled in the rock. Dynamite was set off in the holes, blowing away the unwanted rock. Borglum had to train most of his workers to carve with drills, dynamite and jackhammers. Only a dozen of the 137 workers were previously skilled rock sculptors. Most were Black Hills miners experienced in blasting but not sculpting.

About thirty men worked on the mountain at any one time. They wore masks to keep the rock chips and dust from harming their eyes and lungs. Drillers spread out across each face, with no worker beneath another. This was to avoid injury from dropping debris. Dynamite was set off only at lunch breaks or quitting time. In spite of the many dangers, there was not a single construction death on the project.

Gutzon Borglum worked right along with his crew. He earned the respect and cooperation of the workers, though he was called a slave driver by some. The artist could be extremely demanding of those less committed to the project.

Blasting the stubborn granite was an art Borglum had learned earlier in his career. Dynamite holes were drilled vertically, eight inches apart, as far

Opposite, top: *the four majestic faces of Mount Rushmore are scaled to bodies that would stand 465 feet tall.*

Bottom: *Gutzon Borglum hangs on the face of Rushmore in the swing chair he designed.*

as ten feet into the stone. Early blasts might blow off sixty tons of stone at once. Later holes were less deep and drilled closer together, so that less stone was removed. The crew became so expert they could blast a rounded surface for an eyeball.

Final sculpting was done with a gentle bumping drill plus hammer and chisel. This work was done from cages hung from cables and scaffolding built on the face of the mountain. The finished faces have the texture of concrete pavement.

The four presidents were carved at the same time so they could be adjusted to fit with each other. At first Jefferson was begun on Washington's right, but he didn't fit into the stone there. Then he was moved to Washington's left. The studio model was changed nine times because of flaws in the gray granite mountain.

As the project progressed Borglum was often forced to leave the mountain to solve the worst problem of all: money. By the end of 1927 the original $54,000 had been spent. In 1928 no work was done while Borglum made trips to Washington, D.C., begging Congress to provide money for the memorial. Finally, in 1929, Congress passed the Mount Rushmore bill.

The bill made the Mount Rushmore project a national memorial. It officially named the four faces that are on it today. The bill also directed President Calvin Coolidge to appoint a twelve-member commission to oversee the project. Up to $250,000 was provided, but only if an equal amount was collected from individuals.

Unfortunately, in 1929 America's rosy mood was shattered by the start of the Great Depression. Over 20 percent of Americans were out of work. Most of Mount Rushmore's construction was done during the Depression, and throughout the 1930s the work was stop-and-go because of the difficulty in raising matching funds.

Other difficulties slowed construction as well. There was continual disagreement over whose faces should be on Mount Rushmore. In 1933 Eleanor Roosevelt, wife of President Franklin D. Roosevelt, urged Borglum to include a woman on the mountain. Other concerned women pushed for a congressional bill to add the face of Susan B. Anthony, the famous suffragette. The bill failed in 1936.

While Borglum was in Washington raising money, Lincoln Borglum, his son, supervised the Rushmore carving. Lincoln had worked on it from the beginning, and Borglum trusted his abilities. Borglum finally persuaded Congress to finish the memorial without matching funds, but they did not provide enough money for other parts of the project, including a Hall of Records, which is still not completed.

Above: *Theodore Roosevelt's glasses are mostly optical illusion created by skillful use of light and shadows.*

Above left: *Jefferson's head, nearly completed here, was repositioned many times to avoid a natural crack in the nose.*

Below left: *Herb Conn, Mount Rushmore's "makeup man," inspects Lincoln's face for cracks or damage from weather.*

In March, 1941, with the faces on Mount Rushmore almost finished, Borglum left on a trip to raise money for these other parts of the project. While he was in Chicago, he had surgery for a minor health problem. After the operation, however, Gutzon Borglum died of a heart attack. He was seventy-four.

Lincoln Borglum finished the sculpture on Mount Rushmore in October, 1941. The memorial had cost a little less than the government's 1929 estimate of $1 million. The final cost was $989,992.32, of which Uncle Sam paid some $836,000. The Rushmore project was not really completed, however, because the Hall of Records had barely been started. Lincoln Borglum continued working to get Congress to apportion funds to complete it, and there is hope that someday they will.

Crazy Horse

Built: 1947–
Workers: about 60
Construction deaths: 0
Cost: about $5 million (to 1983)

Mount Rushmore, the Shrine of Democracy, was built as a memorial to all Americans, yet a large part of America went unremembered by it. Women were not included on the mountain, and no mention was ever made of including black Americans.

American Indians were also forgotten on Mount Rushmore, though the very land it stands on was once a sacred burial ground of the Sioux. A few years after Mount Rushmore was finished, Korczak Ziolkowski began to do something about the excluded Indians. Ziolkowski, a self-taught sculptor, had worked as Gutzon Borglum's assistant on Mount Rushmore.

In 1939 Chief Henry Standing Bear, representing the Oglala Sioux, asked Ziolkowski to sculpt an Indian memorial in the Black Hills. Standing Bear wanted the memorial, he said, "so the white man will know the red man had great heroes, too." A vast majority of the Sioux favored a carving of their famous chief, Crazy Horse.

Boston-born Ziolkowski regretted the way the United States government had treated Native Americans. So in 1946 he came to the Black Hills to carve the Crazy Horse memorial at the invitation of Chief Standing Bear.

Model of Ziolkowski's Chief Crazy Horse points to mountain where monument is being carved today.

The chief and Ziolkowski chose Thunderhead Mountain for the Indian sculpture. Thunderhead is seventeen miles from Mount Rushmore. The Sioux organized the Crazy Horse Foundation and bought Thunderhead Mountain from the United States government.

Ziolkowski built a ranch and a sawmill to raise money to support his family and to provide construction funds. He started the sculpture of Crazy Horse in 1947. It is 563 feet high and 641 feet long; four Mount Rushmores would fit on it. In 1982, after carving on the memorial for thirty-five years, Ziolkowski died at the age of seventy-four. Now Ruth Ziolkowski, his wife, and their ten children are finishing it.

No one knows when the Crazy Horse Memorial will be completed. It will be the largest sculpture in the world. Gutzon Borglum, a friend of Korczak Ziolkowski, would surely have admired it. When it is finished, the Crazy Horse Memorial will provide a more complete remembrance of Americans.

9

Big Mac

The Mackinac Bridge

"**P**aper!" shouted the small boy. "Get your paper!" David Steinman sold papers near New York's Brooklyn Bridge. The year was 1896. The bridge was thirteen years old; David was ten.

"How many did you sell?" asked another newsboy later.

"See that bridge?" David asked him, as if he hadn't heard. "I'm going to build bridges like that someday!"

Three years later, at age thirteen, David Steinman entered college to study engineering. He studied bridge building and was awarded a special pass that allowed him to climb the steelwork and watch engineers build the Williamsburg Bridge, a mile and a half up the East River from his beloved Brooklyn Bridge.

At about the same time, nearly a thousand miles away, a bellboy lugged overweight suitcases up the stairs of the Grand Hotel on Mackinac Island. The island, pronounced "Mackinaw," lies in Lake Michigan near the Straits of Mackinac, a four-mile stretch of water that separates the two peninsulas of Michigan.

The ambitious bellhop, Prentiss Brown, was excited. He remembered vividly a picture he had seen of the Brooklyn Bridge in New York City. It had been published in a local newspaper with these words: "A Glimpse of

Built: 1954–1957
Workers: about 1,000
Construction deaths: 5
Cost: about $100 million (or $357 million in 1983)

the Future—Proposed Bridge Across the Straits of Mackinac." A bridge like that seemed an impossible dream in the early 1900s, yet Brown was convinced it was a good idea.

Everyone, including Brown, knew there were tremendous problems to be solved before such a bridge could be built across the straits. In addition to spanning a four-mile gap, the two lakes that meet at the straits are like small oceans.

In winter they come together at Mackinac with a fury! Winds blow west off Lake Huron at over seventy miles an hour; winds just as fierce blow east off Lake Michigan. These gusty foes clash at the straits, often hurling huge ice chunks at each other, piling them up in the waters.

Yet no one doubted that such a bridge was needed. The only way to cross between upper and lower Michigan was by ferry, and the trip took far too long to make regular crossing practical. There must be someone who will know the solution to these problems, Brown thought. But who? And when?

Half a century later, in 1950, David Steinman and Prentiss Brown met. By then Steinman had built nearly four hundred bridges all over the world. Prentiss Brown had become a lawyer, then a United States congressman and senator. He was also chairman of the Mackinac Bridge Authority. There was still no bridge across the straits, but Brown and the authority had chosen Steinman to build one. Other engineers had discussed the usual problems of high winds, too long a span, and the ice. They claimed no bridge could stand these ice fights. Besides, they said, the bedrock beneath the Straits of Mackinac was full of cracks. It would crumble under bridge foundations.

While many people still claimed that building such a bridge was impossible, the fact remained that the only way to cross the straits was by ferry. In 1950 there were eight of these giant ships working there, but they could carry fewer than five hundred vehicles across on each four-mile trip—a trip that took nearly an hour. In the busy summer season cars sometimes had to wait twenty-four hours in a line of traffic twenty miles long.

David Steinman had been testing new bridge designs for seventeen years. He was sure the Straits of Mackinac could be bridged. Because of the high winds it would have to be a suspension bridge, like the Brooklyn Bridge he had known as a boy. It would also have to be built as open as possible so the wind would blow through instead of against it.

To convince the authority and the bridge doubters, Steinman put a model of his bridge in a laboratory wind tunnel. Results showed the bridge could withstand winds of over nine hundred miles per hour.

To solve the bedrock problem Steinman took test drillings from the rock beneath the straits. Though his tests showed the rock was solid, Steinman designed the piers that would support the bridge to be twenty times as strong as needed.

Doubters scoffed as Steinman started building the bridge in May, 1954. In groundbreaking ceremonies Steinman predicted that the bridge would be completed by November, 1957, and cost no more than $100 million. It would carry six thousand vehicles an hour and cut the trip between upper and lower Michigan to ten minutes.

Some 750 workers were hired for the below-water construction of the bridge foundations. The foundations consisted of thirty-two cofferdams and two caissons. The cofferdams were huge steel boxes built on the bottom of the straits. Steel plates were driven into bedrock to form the sides of the boxes. Then the water was pumped out of them and concrete poured in. The resulting steel-and-concrete blocks made platforms—some as high as ten stories—that rose to just above the water's surface. Bridge supports would be built on these.

Two of the biggest cofferdams would serve as cable anchorages. These

Mackinac Bridge Authority

Opposite: *Ice floes on the Straits of Mackinac are finally conquered by the five-mile-long Big Mac.*

Left: *Dr. David B. Steinman, newsboy-turned-bridge builder, conducts an inspection tour of the Mackinac Bridge in August, 1957.*

giant blocks stood at each end of the mile-and-a-half-long suspension section of the bridge. The ends of the suspension cables would be buried in the
anchorages so securely that sixty million pounds of weight couldn't pull
them out.

The two caissons served as foundations for the 527-foot bridge towers.
Each of these caissons was a giant, hollow steel cylinder with sharp edges
and was driven into bedrock more than 100 feet below the straits floor.
They were then filled with layers of crushed rock and concrete, forming

solid piers rising above the water's surface. The bridge towers would be built on the caissons and could support four times the weight of the bridge.

Most of the above-water construction of the bridge was done by Native Americans, who have long been known for their surefootedness in high steel construction. The two bridge towers would eventually rise forty-six stories above the water, so workers could not be afraid of heights.

By the end of 1955 — the second construction season — workers had completed the bridge towers and all the piers. A thousand workers were on the job that year. When an early winter knifed its icy way through the Straits of Mackinac that December, winds slammed the bridge towers in full force at seventy-six miles an hour. Steinman was worried. They had only had time to drive half the rivets that were to hold the towers together. When he inspected them the following spring, however, they stood solidly.

Opposite: *October, 1954: one of the two tower caissons, built on the floor of the straits, is scooped out before being filled with rock and concrete.*

This page: *A steel section of the south tower is raised into place by a "creeper" crane, which is attached to the tower and moves upward as the tower is built.*

In April, 1956, work resumed on the bridge. Fewer workers were needed now, and they began spinning the colossal cables that would support the bridge. First they hung catwalks up to and over the two towers. The catwalks were wire ropes holding up a walkway of chain-link fencing. The men would work from these. Two big spinning wheels moved along wires just above the catwalks, playing out wire behind them.

The spinning wheels ran back and forth over the length of the suspension span, letting out wires for each cable. The wire was as thick as a pencil, and 12,580 wires were spun out for *each* of the two cables. Every 340 wires were squeezed together with a special three-foot pair of pliers to form a single

Workmen turn a giant wrench to bolt the steel girders in place near the south end of the bridge. Photo taken in July, 1956.

strand. The cable makers spun out enough wire to circle the earth's equator nearly twice.

When all the wires for each cable were spun out, they were pressed together—not twisted—with a hydraulic ring press. They were then wrapped with stainless steel wire, making a cable over two feet in diameter. Tension on each wire was carefully adjusted so each cable would do an equal share of holding up the bridge.

After the two main cables were spun, the workers clamped smaller cables to hang down from them about every eighty feet along the main cables. These were the suspender cables, and they would support the steel trusses on

Bridge builders work at incredible heights while squeezing cable with ring press.

Mackinac Bridge Authority

The bridge-to-be during the 1956 construction season, looking south.

which the roadway would be built. The nearly two hundred suspender cables were strong enough to hold up a hundred-mile line of two-ton trucks.

When winter drove the bridge builders away in 1956, almost all the steel trusses that ran from each shore to the suspension span had been put in place. The remaining trusses were ready to be hung on the suspender cables. Work had begun on the roadbed. Though that winter was one of the worst ever, with gale winds slamming ice packs against the bridge and piling them up around its piers, the bridge stood firm.

That winter was also longer than usual and delayed the 1957 construction season. Steinman and his crew would have to hurry if they were to meet their November 1 deadline. The roadway trusses had to be hung on the suspender cables. The road had to be completed and paved. Toll booths had to be put up. Traffic signals and signs would have to be installed, and the bridge still needed its green and ivory paint.

Though some of the roadway was blacktopped just a few days before the opening, the Mackinac Bridge opened on schedule. Cars zipped across the bridge in ten minutes at the speed limit of 45 miles per hour. David Steinman and Prentiss Brown were both at the opening ceremony. The miracul-

THE MACKINAC BRIDGE 77

ous bridge they had dreamed of for years was at last a reality. It was a bridge to be proud of.

"Big Mac" stretches five miles plus forty-four feet from Mackinaw City to St. Ignace, Michigan. It is the longest suspension bridge (measured between anchorages) in the world—and one of the safest, thanks to David Steinman's careful engineering.

Seldom does such a huge construction project cost less than the amount estimated at the beginning. David Steinman, the newsboy-turned-bridge-builder, had met both of his predictions. The bridge opened on schedule, and Big Mac was built for about $99 million—some $1 million less than predicted. Through much hard work by Prentiss Brown and the Mackinac Bridge Authority, bonds had been sold to pay for construction. Tolls are

Roadway trusses are raised from a barge into position at the ends of suspender cables in June, 1957.

Mackinac Bridge Authority

collected from vehicles using the bridge to pay back the borrowed money and to keep the bridge in good repair.

Nowadays two and a half million vehicles cross Big Mac each year. The bond debts should be paid off long before the bridge wears out. Both engineers and contractors admit it is a bridge built to last a thousand years.

Big Mac, one month before completion in 1957.

10

Treasure from Throwaways

The Watts Towers

Built: 1921–1954
Workers: 1
Construction deaths: 0
Cost: about $33,000 (or $125,000 in 1983)

The neighborhood around the Watts Towers looked like a rocket-launching site one Saturday morning in October, 1959. Three hundred people were crowded into short, dead-end 107th Street in Watts, California. Television crews from Los Angeles scurried about, getting ready to televise the scientific test of the Watts Towers, an immense sculpture. The City of Los Angeles had declared the towers unsafe. City officials were afraid the towers might fall on someone or that children might fall while climbing them. The towers would be left standing only if they passed the test.

The tallest tower was about a hundred feet high. Thick cables formed a harness around the tower, with padding between the cables and the tower, so the sculpture wouldn't be harmed. Another cable was attached to this harness and stretched across the Pacific Electric railroad tracks that ran beside the towers. That way if the tower fell, it wouldn't damage any houses. The other end of the cable was run over a pulley attached to a steel beam on the rear of a massive winch truck. The truck driver revved the truck's winch engine, getting ready to wind in the cable and pull on the tower.

Architect Ed Farrell was climbing all over the sculpture, checking the cat-whisker sensors that were taped to the cement-covered steel structure.

The sensors would show how much the tower bent, making it possible to stop the test if the tower started to fall. The architect hoped that the tower would pass the test.

At the foot of the tower, an engineer in a hard hat stood in front of an instrument panel that was wired to measuring devices installed on the tower. These devices would show how many pounds of pull the truck exerted on the tower. The engineer, Norman "Bud" Goldstone, was about to signal the truck operator to pull on the cable. Goldstone had designed this test and was sure the tower would hold up.

Those people in the crowd who thought the towers were a hazard carried signs that said, UNSAFE. Other people in the crowd disagreed with them; they carried signs that read, THE WATTS TOWERS BELONG TO THE PEOPLE. Some of these people were members of the Committee for Rodia's Towers in Watts, which had been formed to save the towers from destruction. The committee had arranged this test with architect Farrell and engineer Goldstone to prove that the towers were safe.

"Everybody back!" shouted Bud Goldstone as the winch truck began to pull on the tower.

Soon Goldstone announced, "Thirty percent of load!" The truck continued to pull. The pull on the tower would have to be increased to ten thousand pounds—equal to the force of a seventy-mile-an-hour wind—in order for the towers to be proved safe and allowed to remain standing.

Ed Farrell climbed about on the tower, checking the sensors.

"Approaching forty percent load!" Goldstone called out.

One person in the crowd was watching the test especially closely. He was Harold Manley, chief of the Los Angeles Building and Safety Department's Conservation Bureau. It was Manley's responsibility to have the towers torn down, but the demolition had been delayed. Manley had often called the towers a pile of junk, and was hoping to bring this matter to a close.

"One hundred percent load!" shouted Goldstone. The tower was still standing—only one tiny seashell had fallen from it. Still, the tower would have to withstand the full pull of ten thousand pounds for five minutes in order to be declared safe. That had been the agreement between the City of Los Angeles and the Committee for Rodia's Towers in Watts.

After one and a half minutes, the tip of the tower had leaned sideways only an inch and a quarter. Suddenly the beam holding the cable on the winch truck began to bend! The test was stopped. Slowly Harold Manley—enemy of the Watts Towers—picked up one of the UNSAFE signs. He walked over to engineer Goldstone and handed him the sign.

Opposite: *The graceful towers of Sam Rodia in Watts, California. Shadows change the towers' appearance minute by minute.*

"That's long enough to prove the towers' strength," said Manley. "I'm on your side now."

Cheers went up from those in the crowd who were in favor of letting the towers stand. The people who had wanted them torn down went away disappointed. The Watts Towers would be left standing.

The sculptor who had built the towers, Sam Rodia—sometimes called Simon—was not there that day. Sam Rodia was an Italian immigrant who came to the United States as a boy sometime around 1890. He found jobs as a common laborer on construction projects and worked his way across the country to California by the early 1900s. Settling in Martinez, California, Rodia married and had three children. Then he separated from his wife and family and moved to southern California. By the 1920s he had settled in Watts, in south Los Angeles. He bought a house on a tiny three-cornered lot and began building his towers.

The short, thinly built Rodia was once asked why he built the towers. "I had in mind to do something big," he answered, "and I did." The Watts Towers are the largest work of art ever created by one person. Those amazing towers of Mr. Rodia, which refused to be pulled down in 1959, are built of steel and cement—and throwaways. To construct them Rodia collected broken bottles, dishes, cups, seashells, pieces of tile—anything people didn't want or threw away.

Rodia bought some of the materials he used, such as cement, sand and steel for the understructure. He used seven thousand sacks of waterproof cement in his construction. The sculptor also purchased some of the hundreds of broken dishes for the towers. He gave neighborhood children a penny apiece for them, as well as for some of the tiles he used. He paid for these from his earnings as a full-time construction worker and night watchman in the Los Angeles area.

Sam Rodia worked alone, using only the simplest of tools—and he used no bolts, rivets or welds. He bent the structural steel for the towers beneath the rails of the nearby railroad tracks. He buried the towers' metal "feet" 14 inches into the ground for a foundation. Working upward, he overlapped the steel rods, fastened them with wire and covered this with wire mesh. Then he hand packed cement on top of the wire mesh. The steel plus wire plus cement made joints so strong that the truck couldn't pull them apart more than thirty-five years after the first ones were completed.

The greatest achievement of Rodia's towers is not their strength, however, but their beauty. One modern-day artist has called Sam Rodia's towers "a song he built that is still singing." Sam Rodia created this beauty out of

A rare photograph of Sam Rodia during the final years of work on the construction of his masterpiece.

Both photos this page: Dan Ward, The Committee for Rodia's Towers in Watts

everything from bits of broken colored glass to a bowling ball pressed into the wet cement. The result is a fascinating rainbow of mosaic designs. Viewing the Watts Towers is like looking into a kaleidoscope.

From a distance Rodia's creation looks like a sailing ship, with the three tallest towers as the masts. A 7-foot-high wall forms a triangle around the "masts," with two legs—150 feet long—forming the sides of the ship, and a third leg—about 75 feet long—looking like the back of the ship. In fact, Rodia named the three towers after the ships of one of his favorite heroes, Christopher Columbus: the *Niña,* the *Pinta* and the *Santa Maria.*

There are seven towers altogether, and none of them was constructed like any of the others. Of the three tallest, one looks like a stack of giant drums, another like a huge flowerpot and the third like a colossal birdcage.

Up close, flowers, hearts and curlicues burst out everywhere from the towers. They are blended into eye-pleasing patterns. The base of the tallest tower is covered with chopped multicolored glass in a crazy-quilt design. The base of the second tallest tower is decorated with dozens of seashells set in straight rows. The next tallest tower's base is inlaid with a lively collage of broken bathroom tiles.

Left: *many decorative panels as this one made of pieces of tile and curlicues, line the walls surrounding the Watts Towers.*

Right: *Rodia used a special technique to make this design, created by inverting a mold over the wet cement to make a raised, rather than inverted picture.*

On this panel Rodia pressed the tools he used into the wet cement.

On the inside of the walls surrounding the towers, Sam Rodia pressed the imprints of odds and ends he picked up in junkyards. On one wall is the outline of an old-fashioned sewing machine cover, for example. Next to that is the imprint of a bunch of wax grapes, a straw basket, some automobile gears and a stem of wheat. Bulging out from the wall are cement shapes of corncobs and old boots. Another design on the walls is made up of broken pieces of china dogs and squirrels. All these bits and pieces were carefully arranged by Rodia into what the New York Museum of Modern Art has called "a unique creation of inspiring power and beauty, a masterpiece of assemblage."

One design on the outside of the wall shows the outlines of the tools Rodia used. There are several hammers, two files, a pair of pliers, screwdrivers and a chisel. He made no advance blueprints for the construction. He used the day-by-day ideas that grew out of his own creative mind. Rodia's construction work skills served him well.

There are many steel spokes sticking out from the towers that connect them to each other and to the walls. These spokes form a web of metal and give the towers their great strength. Buckminster Fuller, the architect, once

Right: *after completing a panel, Rodia sometimes worked the year of its completion into the design. This one is dated 1923.*

Below left: *the rose design in the walls of Sam Rodia's towers was made by pressing a water faucet handle into the wet cement.*

Below right: *Rodia pressed hundreds of bottles like these into the tower sculpture.*

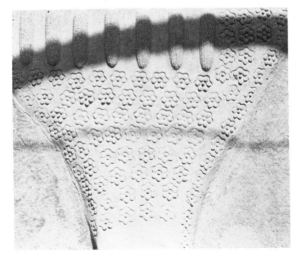

said that Rodia's towers were built as a tree grows, ring by ring. The many steel rings around each tower give them what modern engineers call *redundancy,* which is the repeating of supports in a structure, adding strength.

By 1954 Sam Rodia, whose Italian name was Sabatino Rodia, was well into his seventies. He had worked thirty-three years on his towers and was worried about his health. Los Angeles city officials were beginning to badger him for building without a permit. Rumors around Rodia's neighborhood said that there was money hidden behind the objects he had cemented onto the towers. Children smashed the shells and bottles with rocks and even broke into Rodia's house while he was away at night. Rodia was heartbroken. The once-friendly sculptor became a hermit for a while. Finally he sold his property to a neighbor, Louis Sauceda, and moved to northern California, leaving his towers behind.

At first no one knew where Rodia had gone after abandoning the almost-completed towers. Five years later he was found living in Martinez, California, four hundred miles north of Los Angeles. He refused to have anything to do with the towers for the rest of his life. He never returned to see his masterpiece. Sam Rodia died in 1965.

Before his death, when friends visited Rodia in Martinez, he would not even talk about the towers. "If your mother dies and you have loved her very much," he told them, "maybe you don't speak of her." Something Sam Rodia had loved dearly—the towers—had been nearly destroyed; by 1959 the towers' beautiful designs were in disrepair. The City of Los Angeles had condemned the towers to be demolished.

That same year William Cartwright, a young film editor from Los Angeles, visited the Watts Towers and recognized them as an art treasure. Such beauty, he thought, must be saved from destruction. He soon brought a movie-actor friend, Nicholas King, to see the towers, and together they bought them for $3,000 from a local businessman who had purchased them from Rodia's neighbor. The two men formed the Committee for Rodia's Towers in Watts to preserve the monument. The committee was made up of some thirty artists, architects, lawyers, students and others who wanted to save the towers. They began to raise money for this project.

The community of Watts was a troubled black ghetto of thirty-four thousand people. Family incomes there were only half as high as the incomes of other Los Angeles families. The neighborhood, ten miles from the center of Los Angeles, was cut off from the rest of the city because it had no bus service, and many people in Watts could not afford cars. This situation led to the Watts Riots of 1965, when angry blacks revolted, demanding a better life. Businesses in Watts were destroyed and thirty-five people were killed.

William Cartwright and Nicholas King believed the Watts Towers might bring a sense of community pride to the people of Watts. The committee Cartwright and King had formed raised thousands of dollars to fight the City of Los Angeles and save the construction. They won the fight in 1959, when the towers passed the structural safety test. Soon the City of Los Angeles declared the Watts Towers a cultural heritage monument.

During the early 1960s many black artists from Los Angeles visited the monument in Watts. They sketched and painted pictures of Rodia's masterpiece. Neighborhood children watched at first, then joined in the sketching and painting. From that beginning the towers committee started free art classes for the children of Watts. There were also drama classes and exhibits of the works of artists and photographers from all over the United States. In 1970 the Committee for Rodia's Towers in Watts raised money and built an art center building. Today there are classes at the center in art, crafts, music and dance, and poetry. The center has become a hub of creativity and culture in the Watts community.

Every year some sixty thousand visitors come from all over the world to see the Watts Towers. The state of California is spending several million dollars to restore this cultural heritage monument to its original condition. Because it is being preserved, visitors can see the beauty of Rodia's masterpiece as he created it.

All over the walls and towers that Rodia built are hundreds of roses. Rodia created these bouquets by pressing the handle of an outdoor water faucet into the wet cement. Jeanne Morgan, an artist who was a founding member of the towers committee, has described the beauty of Sam Rodia's work. "Rodia saw beauty in everything," she said. "He looked at the handle of a water faucet and he saw a rose."

Sam Rodia used people's throwaways to construct a work of art they would treasure forever. The United States Congress has placed Rodia's towers on the National Register of Historic Monuments, the list of America's greatest treasures.

Index

Anasazi Indians, 4–10
Ancon (ship), 37, 44, 45

Bartholdi, Frédéric-Auguste, 29, 30–33, 35
Bedloe's Island, 30, 33, 36
Black Canyon, 53, 54, 56, 57, 59
Black Hills, 62
Borglum, Gutzon, 61–62, 63–64, 66
Borglum, Lincoln, 64, 66
Boulder City, Nevada, 56–57, 60

Caisson (steel) construction, 48–49, 50, 70–72, 73
Cliff dwellings, 3–10
  abandoned, 10
  construction of, 7–8
  location of, 3
Cliff Palace, 8, 9
Colorado River, 53, 55, 57, 60
Committee for Rodia's Towers, 81, 87, 88
Crazy Horse Memorial, 66–67
Crowe, Frank, 55–56, 58, 59
Cumberland, Maryland, 11, 12, 13, 20
Cumberland Road, 18–19

Eiffel, Gustave, 33

Freeman, Milton, 50

Goethals, George Washington, 2, 37, 40–43, 46
Gorgas, Dr. William, 39, 42

Holland, Clifford M., 46–47, 50, 51, 52
Holland Tunnel, 46–52
  air-lock tubes, 50
  caissons, 48–49, 50
  height and width of, 48
  length of, 52
  opening day ceremony, 51
  shield tunnel construction, 47–51
  ventilation problems, 50

Hoover Dam, 2, 53–60
  completion of, 59, 60
  Congress and, 55
  construction of, 56–59
  electrical power, 59–60
  how it works, 60

Jefferson, Thomas, 12, 13, 18
  face on Mount Rushmore, 61, 62, 64, 65
Jersey City, New Jersey, 46

Know-Nothings, 24–25

Laboulaye, Edouard, 30–31
Lincoln, Abraham, 23
  face on Mount Rushmore, 61, 62, 65
Long House cliff dwelling, 3, 4
Los Angeles, California, 79, 81, 82, 87, 88

Mackinac Bridge, 68–78
  bedrock problem, 70
  construction of, 70–76
  foundation, 70–72
  length of, 77
  opening ceremony, 76–77
  suspension cables, 72, 74–76
  tolls, 77–78
Mackinaw City, Michigan, 77
Marshall, John, 21, 22
Martinez, California, 82, 87
Mesa Verde cliff dwellings, 3–10
Mills, Robert, 23
Mount Rushmore, 61–67
  completion of, 66
  Congress and, 64, 66
  faces on, 61, 62, 65–66
  Hall of Records, 64, 66
  idea for, 62
  money problems, 64
  sculpting and construction of, 62–64
Mount Vernon, Virginia, 22

National Register of Historic Monuments, 88

National Road, 11–20
    completion of, 17
    Congress and, 12–13, 17, 19
    extension of, 18, 20
    first ten miles, 16–17
    length of, 11, 13–14
    map of, 13
    pavement, 15–16, 18–19, 20
    renamed, 20
    use of immigrant labor, 14–15, 16
    western section of, 18–19
Native Americans, 23, 66–67; *See also*
    names of tribes

Oglala Sioux Indians, 66–67

Panama Canal, 2, 37–45, 46
    Congress and, 40
    construction of, 38, 39–44
    first person to swim, 44–45
    immigrant workers, 42
    locks, 40, 42, 43–44, 45
    opening day ceremony, 44, 45
    ownership of, 45
    ship tolls, 44
Philadelphia, Pennsylvania, 33
Pueblo Indians, 4, 10
Pulitzer, Joseph, 33

Red Cloud, Chief, 62
Robinson, Doane, 62
Rodia, Sam, 82–84, 85, 87, 88
Roosevelt, Franklin D., 60, 64
Roosevelt, Theodore, 38, 39, 40, 42
    face on Mount Rushmore, 61, 62, 65

St. Ignace, Michigan, 77
St. Louis, Missouri, 13, 18, 19
Shriver, David, 14, 15
Singstad, Ole, 50, 51
Sioux Indians, 62, 66–67
Standing Bear, Chief Henry, 66
Statue of Liberty, 29–36
    Congress and, 33
    construction of, 31–33, 34
    height of, 30
    idea for, 31
    meaning of, 35–36
    poem (on the pedestal), 35
    renovations and repairs, 36
    unveiling ceremony, 29–30, 33–35

Steinman, David B., 68, 69–70, 73, 76–77
Stevens, John "Big Smoke," 39–40, 42
Straits of Mackinac, 68, 69, 73

United States Congress, 12–13, 17, 19, 21,
    22, 23–24, 33, 40, 55, 64, 66, 88

Vandalia, Illinois, 11, 19, 20

Wallace, John, 39, 42
Washington, D.C., 13, 19, 27
Washington, George, 12, 21, 22, 23, 25, 28
    face on Mount Rushmore, 61, 62, 64
Washington Monument, 21–28
    capstone, 26, 27
    completion of, 27
    Congress and, 21, 22, 23–24
    construction of, 23–27
    cornerstone ceremony, 23, 28
    design, 22–23
    foundation, 22, 25–26
    fund raising for, 23, 24, 25
    height of, 26
    marble ring around, 26
    proposal for, 21
Wattis, Edmund, 2, 55, 59
Watts Ghetto (California), 79, 87
Watts Towers, 79–88
    condemned, 87
    creation, construction, and design of,
        82–87
    saved from destruction, 87–88
    scientific testing of, 79–81, 88
Wilson, Woodrow, 43

Young, Walker, 55–56, 58, 59

Ziolkowski, Korczak, 66–67
Ziolkowski, Ruth, 67